Indian Economy and Reforms

Strictly on the basis of prescribed syllabus with modern trends

Indian Economy and Reforms

Strictly on the basis of prescribed syllabus with modern trends

Charu Arora

AUTHORSPRESS

Worldwide Circulation through Authorspress Global Network
First Published 2008
by
Authorspress
E-35/103, Jawahar Park
Laxmi Nagar, Delhi-110 092
e-mail: authorspress@yahoo.com

Indian Economy and Reforms
ISBN 978-81-7273-431-2

Printed in India at Virgo Press, Delhi.

Foreword

Students of journalism and mass communication always have reservations about studying non-media papers at the undergraduate level. But in almost all journalism and mass communication programmes non-media papers have been prescribed in the first year itself. BJ (MC) programme of Guru Gobind Singh Indraprastha University and Journalism Hons programme of Delhi University both have political science and economics papers in the first year. Reservation of students apart the decision makers and course designers always brainstorm as to what should exactly be taught under political science and economic papers. Taking a decision on course contents of these papers is a challenge, which needs to be taken up in view of different requirements of media students.

In GGS IP University we tried to address the different need of media students by replacing 'State and Politics' paper, by 'Indian Government and Politics' and Social History' paper by 'Indian Economy and Reforms' at the time of syllabi revision in the year 2005. Prof Saroj Aggarwal as Director, Academic Affairs and I as Course Coordinator of BJ (MC) programme, became instrumental updating the syllabus in a manner that subjects like Indian economy become the favourite of students. 'Indian Economy and Reforms' paper was designed to include all major developments in Indian Economy in post liberalisation era.

Educationists will agree with me that simply making a good syllabus can bear no fruits if the delivery system is not good. This was reminded to me by both Prof Devesh Kishore, Dean, Institute of Management Studies, Noida [Former Head-Education and Training, EMPC, IGNOU] and Prof Pradeep Mathur, Course

Director, Journalism, Indian Institute of Mass Communication, when I was designing the Course curriculum of Master of Mass Media (MMM) programme in May-June this year. In media education, task is comparatively more difficult as there is a real dearth of good teachers. If there are no good people around who can do justice with media papers, then where to search for teachers capable of handling non-media papers with a media perspective. As education administrator I have involved in this search but meeting with Charu Arora has led me to think that there are solutions to problems.

Charu is among these few teachers who have impressed me. As Director of Vivekananda Institute of Professional Studies (VIPS) I was looking for a teacher who could teach the newly introduced paper "Indian Economy and Reforms" to BJ (MC) students in 2005 and my search ended at Charu. She accepted the challenge despite all her teaching load in BCA and did justice to the assignment. In 2006 also she came forward to take up the paper despite the fact that it meant an extra load. Charu is a brilliant student and excellent teacher who is honest to her profession and this is what has made me her admirer.

Charu is young and vibrant and you can always find energy oozing out while she is at work. She is pretty and charming who is mostly mixed up with young girl students but when it comes to professional appearance, she is distinctly noticed. So, when Charu told me recently that she was working on a book on Indian Economy for the journalism students I was not much surprised. I knew she could do the job. She showed me the manuscript and I gave her relevant suggestions. Soon she was ready with the final draft and we started searching for a publisher. And the search ended at Authorspress.

I have edited a business magazine M & M for many years and have been anchoring a business programme 'Market Mantra' on AIR FM Gold for the last six years, and with that experience I can say it with authority that this is undoubtedly the best and the most update book on fundamentals and reforms in Indian Economy. The book deals with mostly post liberalisation developments, policy shifts and the impact on various sectors. Right from Exim, FDI and FII to privatisation and disinvestment, the book carries material of direct use to students.

The book deals with all such sectors, which are vital for economy, infrastructure, financial and banking. The material on infrastructure development-energy, transport, communication attracts attention. The author has dealt with reforms in banking, capital market and taxation carrying all necessary details and latest developments. And no doubt chapter on WTO is a value addition.

I am sure that this book will act as a friend to all undergraduate students of journalism and mass communication in Guru Gobind Singh Indraprastha University, Delhi University and elsewhere. This book is no less valuable to non-media students if they have a paper on Indian Economy as part of their curriculum. Even for those who want to understand intricate issues of economy, and wish to have a clear picture of the performance of Indian Economy, this book can serve as a basic document on the subject. My best wishes for the success of this endeavour.

Prof. Ambrish Saxena
Consultant, Centre for Media Studies
GGS IP University, Delhi

Preface

With great pleasure, I present my book, *Indian Economy and Reforms*, written strictly in accordance with the syllabus prescribed for the students of Bachelor of Journalism and Mass Communication, Guru Govind Singh Indraprastha University. The book is a sincere endeavour to provide to the students a textbook with extensive coverage of the prescribed reading list.

Even while making use of statistical data, necessary precautions have been taken not to burden the students with unnecessary and avoidable statistical details. The whole idea has been to make the presentation of the subject fully authentic yet easy to understand and simple to grasp.

Charu Arora

Acknowledgement

My special thanks to Ms. Anuradha Jain for supporting me with her ideas and I am grateful to Mr. Amrish Saxena for his help in bringing this book forward.

I appreciate the help of Harish, Mitika, Bhawna and Neha for contributing towards the collection of data for the book.

I am also grateful to Divya, Mayank, Aneesh and Abhishek for their assistance in typing and formatting the book.

Charu Arora

Contents

1

An Introduction to Indian Economy

MEANING AND CONCEPT OF ECONOMICS

Different economists have given different definitions of economics. These definitions are liable to undergo change with changing times and conditions. It is so because subject matter of economics is ever changing. According to Lord Robbins", Economics is a science that studies human behavior as a relationship between ends and scarce means which have alternative uses."

According to Adam Smith, economics is a study of wealth. It is a narrow and unscientific definition of economics as it put more emphasis on wealth than man. Actually, wealth is simply a means to satisfy man's wants. Dr. Marshall was of the opinion that "it examines that part of individual and social action which is most closely connected with the attainment and with the use of material requisites of well-being."

Features of Economics

1. Unlimited Wants or Ends

By "ends," Lord Robbins means wants in economics. We study those wants, which are concerned with goods and services. These are known as Economic Wants There is no limit to these wants. This chain of wants is endless. As one want is satisfied, immediately another crops up.

2. Limited or Scarce Means

Means are referred to as resources, which are used for satisfying wants. These means are scarce, i.e., their demand is more than the supply.

3. Alternative uses of means

The major economic problem is that these scarce means have alternative uses. Milk, we know, is a means. It can be used for preparing butter, curd, cheese, etc.

4. Wants differ in urgency

Man has several wants, but at any given time one of these wants may be more urgent and important than other wants.

5. Opportunity cost

Lord Robbins' definition tells us that it is due to the problem of choice that in order to fulfil one want we have to forego another. We cannot fulfil all our wants simultaneously.

Therefore, economy can be defined as, "orderly arrangement and management of the internal affairs of a state or of any establishment kept up by production and consumption; especially such management as directly concerns wealth; as political economy."

Economy is

1. A system of production and distribution and consumption,
2. Efficient use of resources,
3. Frugality in the expenditure of money or resources, and
4. An act of economising; reduction in cost.

People go to work in farms, factories, banks, hospitals, schools, hotels, etc., in order to earn income. Such activities are called Economic Activities. Like individuals, government also does some economic activities by engaging people in various jobs. When all these economic activities are carried out in a framework, it is called an Economy. There are many other activities, which do not give any income in return, they are called Non-Economic Activities. When an activity results in a valuable and useful thing, it is called Production of Goods. Production may range from a simple safety pin to sophisticated aircrafts.

Activities such as transportation, medical treatment, postal services, courier and telephone booths, haircut, washing of clothes, etc., are considered as Production of Services. When people use goods and services, it is called Consumption.

All economic activities are classified into three categories – Primary, Secondary and Tertiary Activities.

Activities that are associated directly with land and water such as farming, rearing of cattle, hunting, fishing and mining, etc are called Primary Activities. In this segment, goods are either grown or dig out of the earth. All the goods produced in this way are primary goods such as wheat, vegetables, marble, coal, etc.

When primary goods are used to produce some other commodities manually or by machines, then the activity is known as Secondary Activity. It is also known as Manufacturing. For instance, paper from wood, bread from wheat, steel bars from iron, etc. There is some mutual dependency between primary and secondary activities. For both primary and secondary activities, we require a substantial amount of support services. For instance, to produce bread, we use wheat. To take wheat from the field to the factory, we use transport. We also use transport to take bread from factory to the consumers. Such support activities are known as Tertiary Activities. All those activities that link the producers and the consumers come under tertiary activities. They are also known as service activities such as retail distribution shops, wholesale distribution shops, banks, etc.

In order to carry out various economic activities, some amount of resources are required. In economic terms, these are called Inputs or Factors of Production, because they help in production of various commodities. In general, land, labour, capital and organisation are called the factors of production. These are also known as resources that are owned by individuals, community, government or combinations of any two or three.

On the basis of ownership of resources, economies are classified into three types:

1. Capitalist or free market economy
2. Socialist or command economy
3. Mixed economy

CAPITALISM

The capitalist system is one characterised by the private ownership of the means of production, individual decision-making of participants and facilitates the flow of goods and services in the markets. Under the capitalist system, the means of production land, labour and capital are under the ownership of individuals. The owner of these means use them for their maximum advantage. Workers on the other hand, are free to choose their occupation and place of work. The owner of the means of production, the capitalist, is also free to choose the workers on his terms. Since the capitalist is in a superior position *vis-à-vis* the worker, the workers are forced to sell their labour to the capitalist on terms suiting the latter.

Capitalism may be further divided into:

a) Laissez-faire economies where government intervention in the working of the economy is negligible.

b) Mixed capitalist where there is substantial amount of government intervention.

Features of Capitalist Economy

1. *Private ownership of means of production:* The factors of production – land, capital—is owned privately and individually by members of the economic system. Every individual has a right to acquire property, keep it, and pass it on to his heirs.

2. *Individual initiative:* Production is carried out at the initiative of the individuals and is not subject to or controlled by the government. The individuals take their decision on the basis of the market conditions.

3. *Objective pursued: Maximise private gains*: All individuals in the capitalist system are motivated and guided by objective of maximising private gains. Producers are guided by objective of maximising profits, workers want to maximise their income and consumers want maximum satisfaction from the commodities they purchase and consume.

4. *Economic freedom:* Under capitalism each individual enjoys the freedom to excercise his own initiative in taking

decisions. As a producer, the individual is free to use his means of production to produce and sell any commodity. As a consumer, he is free to make his own purchases and consume the goods so purchased in the manner he likes.

5. *Presence of economic rivalry or competition:* Since self-interest and private gains guide each individual, there exists economic rivalry among sellers, among buyers, potential workers, and so on. Competition among sellers forces them to optimally use their means of production and produce the given output at the minimum cost.
6. *Market mechanism or price mechanism:* The problems of "what to produce, how to produce and for whom to produce" are solved in a capitalist economy using the price mechanism. The production and distribution of all goods and services is entrusted to market forces (i.e., demand and supply) rather than to the rules and regulations of the centrally planned economy.
7. *Limited role of the government:* The role of the government in the working of the economy is limited to general administration, defence and protect property rights, maintain law and order and protection from external aggression. The government does not interfere in the free working of the economy.
8. *Class-based society:* Capitalism results in a class-based society. The capitalist society is divided into two groups: the capitalists (the haves) and the workers (the have nots). The capitalists are the owners of means of production and employ workers to produce goods and services.

Socialism

Socialism is an economic organisation of society in which the material means of production are owned by the whole community according to a general economic plan, all members being entitled to the benefit from the results of such socialised planned production on the basis of equal rights.

The means of production are owned and managed by the state and all decisions w.r.t. the working of the economy – what to produce, how to produce, for whom to produce, etc., – are taken by the state. The state is guided by the objective of maximising social benefit.

Features of Socialist System

1. *Social ownership of the means of production:* The means of production are owned and managed by the state. This is also known as Collective Ownership. The economic activities are guided by the objective set by the state, as defined in the central economic plans.
2. *Central economic planning:* Planning is a must under socialism. This is because all economic activities have to be determined and coordinated through a central plan. The economy, therefore, has a central planning authority that formulates the plan for the entire economy.
3. *Specified objectives:* All economic activities undertaken in this kind of system are guided by predetermined social and economic motives. Some of the objectives may concern employment levels, amount of capital accumulation, distribution of national output, economic growth, etc.
4. *Absence of profit-motive and elimination of economic rivalry*: Profit objective is replaced by social objective under socialism. There is absence of wasteful competition among producers. Competition is replaced by cooperation.
5. *No class-based division of society:* Socialism aims for a society in which there are no inequalities of income and wealth. It tries to minimise the gap between the rich and the poor.

Mixed Economic System

A mixed economy is a compromise between capitalism and socialism. It combines the features of both the capitalist and the socialist. It tries to bring together the advantages of both capitalism and socialism without the demerits of either. In the mixed economy, there is the coexistence of the public and private sector. The public sector consists of those industrial and service units that are controlled and managed by state. The industries that are reserved for the public sector are generally of strategic importance – commonly referred to as heavy and basic industries. The private sector consists of all the business units that are owned and managed by private individuals and institutions. Industrial units in the private sector are guided by the objectives of self-interest, private gains and profit maximisation. The public sector, on the other hand, is guided by socio-economic objectives determined in the plans formulated by the state.

Features of a Mixed Economy

1. *Co-existence of public and private sector:* The public sector is created by the state by reserving certain industries, to be managed and controlled by the state itself. Industries included in the public sector are those, which are of strategic importance to the economy. Industries requiring huge investments, having long gestation periods and low profitability are generally operated under the public sector, e.g., power generation, posts and telegraphs, etc.

   In the private sector, the business units are owned and managed by private individuals. Private sector is not allowed to produce those goods and services that are to be produced exclusively by the public sector. The working of the private sector is, however, controlled by the state through laws, rules and regulations. The private sector has to operate within the framework of these rules and regulations.

2. *Economic planning:* It involves the conceiving, initiating, regulating and controlling the economic activities by the state, according to set priorities, with a view to achieve specific and well-defined objectives within a given time period. Therefore, the economic plans act as instruments of direction, control and regulation of economic activities carried on in the economy.

3. *Profit motive and social interest:* The private sector is guided by the profit motive but also has certain social responsibilities to perform that are in the interest of society. The public sector is guided by the objective of social interest and social welfare.

4. *Economic freedom and control:* Consumers enjoy the freedom of consumption, private producers enjoy the freedom of production and private individuals enjoy the freedom to purchase and hold property. However, the state does impose regulations and control over the economic activities.
5. *Social welfare functions:* The state undertakes the function of increasing the social welfare of the economy. To protect the different sections of society, the state formulates and implements various laws. Laws related to safeguarding the interests of workers, consumers, and general public are passed by the legislature. The aim is to prevent the exploitation of different categories of individuals and promote social welfare of the economy as a whole.

Therefore, in the public sector, the state decides what to produce, for whom to produce, etc., through the formulation of economic plans. The state in making these decisions are guided by the needs of the economy and social interest. In the private sector, the decision of "what to produce" is indirectly influenced by the policies of the state. Thus, the state regulates the free working of price mechanism through its industrial, fiscal, monetary policies and also through direct controls. Economic planning on one hand and state intervention in the working of the price mechanism on the other, solves the basic problems of the mixed economy.

Impediments to Development

Economic development is of utmost significance to all economies. It is necessary for underdeveloped countries because they can solve the problems of general poverty, unemployment, backwardness and low standard of living through it. On the other hand, it is equally significant to developed economies as it helps them to maintain their existing growth rate. Although Adam Smith, the father of modern economics, had examined the problem of economic development two hundred years ago, yet it is only for the last 60 years that economists took great interest in the study of the problems of underdeveloped countries. It may be noted that the term "Economic Development" and "Economic Growth" are used interchangeably. But economists make a distinction between them. Economic development means growth with change and increase in welfare.

There are number of different ways in which the economies of the world are categorised. The World Development Report has classified the economies of the world on the basis of their per capita income in the following three categories:

— High-income economies are those with a per capita income of 9,265 dollars or more.

— Middle-income economies are those with a per capita income of more than 755 dollars but less than 9,265 dollars.

— Low-income economics are those with a per capita income of 755 dollars or less.

The low-income economies are also referred to as Underdeveloped Economies. About three-fourths of the world's population lives in these economies. These are characterised by poverty, ignorance and disease. On the other hand, high-income countries are termed as Advanced Countries. Only one-fourth of the world's population lives in these economies. These are characterised by high standard of living and high expectancy of life. However, the above-mentioned economies of the world have been called by many different names. One is Backward and Advances Economies or Traditional and Modern ones. On the basis of their development, they may be underdeveloped and developed countries, or developing and developed countries.

The concept of economic growth refers to quantitative changes. It is a process of growth in the national and per capita income. The concept of economic development is something more than of the economic growth. It refers to growth in real per capita income as well as structural institution change and increase in economic welfare or well being of the people.

Basic Hindrances in Economic Development

India is an underdeveloped though a developing economy. The bulk of the population lives in conditions of misery. Poverty is not only acute but also chronic. At the same time, there exist unutilised natural resources. The co-existence of the vicious circle of poverty with the vicious circle of affluence perpetuates misery and roils all attempts at removal of poverty. It is in this context that an understanding of the major issues of development should be made. The following are the major development issues in India.

Low Per Capita Income and Low Rate of Economic Growth

In the years since 1950 the developed countries have improved their per capita income at a much faster rate but India has been limping along so badly. Barring a few countries in the world, the per capita income of the Indian people is the lowest in the world.

High Proportion of People Below Poverty Line

A major development issue is the removal of mass poverty. Indian economy indicates a very high proportion of people below the poverty line. The burden of poverty is very massive. Rapid reduction and eventually the elimination of poverty is, therefore, the most important issue of development.

Low Level of Productive Efficiency Due to Inadequate Nutrition and Malnutrition

The National Sample Survey has estimated that about 56 per cent of the urban population and about 49 per cent of the rural population suffer from inadequate nutrition, as they do not get a calorie intake of 2,400 per day considered as a reasonable level of nutrition. The level of malnutrition in all expenditure groups was higher in the urban areas than in the rural areas. Nutrition influences economic development via raising the level of productivity, efficiency and intelligence of the community.

Imbalance between Population Size, Resources and Capital

A very important problem, which affects economic development is the rapid growth of population. A rising population imposes greater economic burden and, consequently, society has to make a much greater effort to initiate the process of growth. Moreover, with a rising population, per capita availability of land and such other resources fixed in supply, declines. Therefore, checking the fast growth of population has a close relationship with economic development.

Problem of Unemployment

A major development issue in India is to eliminate unemployment and provide gainful employment to millions of people without work. The development plans in India have failed to absorb even the normal increase in labour force, not to speak of reducing the backlog of unemployment.

Instability of Output of Agriculture and Related Sectors

One of the major problems of Indian economy is the uncertainty of agricultural production, since agriculture is still a gamble in the monsoons. Since independence, there has been considerable increase in the production of the agricultural sector. In spite of this spectacular growth, food grains output has been fluctuating from year to year. This is also true of oilseeds, sugarcane, cotton and jute-the major commercial crops. Instability of output of agriculture also results in causing instability in the related sectors. Thus, a major development issue for the Indian economy is to devise a strategy of agricultural development, which can promise a steady growth of agricultural output.

Inequalities in Distribution of Income and Wealth

With the increase in the concentration of income and wealth, the inequalities are also rising simultaneously. The condition of the bottom 20 percent of the population has definitely deteriorated and the next 20 percent has remained stagnant. Therefore, there is a need to assure continuous growth with economic justice through better distribution of income and wealth.

To sum up, all these issues of economic development should be given due importance. Solutions should be worked out in order to overcome from these obstacles so as to make India move at a faster growth rate.

NATURE OF INDIAN ECONOMY

Underdeveloped countries are those that have real per capita income less than a quarter of the per capita income of United States. UN publications, instead of referring them as underdeveloped, describe them as 'developing economies'. By this they mean that though still underdeveloped, yet the process of development has been initiated in these countries. India has one-fourth population that lives in conditions of misery. The problem of poverty is not only acute but chronic. There exist unutilised natural resources.

Low Per Capita Income

According to Prof. Kurihara, "Low per capita Real Income is the chief characteristic of an underdeveloped economy." Per capita income of India is less than that of most of the countries in the world. Nonetheless, Indian economy is growing at a faster rate as compared to developed economies. But still the difference between the per capita income of India and developed countries is very large. In USA the per capita income is 68 dollars. As against India, the per capita income in USA is 68 times more, in UK it is 50 times more and in Japan, it is 75 times more. Attempts are being made to narrow down these differences – official exchange rates and purchasing power parity.

Occupational Pattern

One of the major problem is that 61 per cent of working population is engaged in agriculture, out of it only 28 per cent contributes to national income. The problem of population engaged in agriculture in developed countries is much less than the problem of population engaged in agriculture in underdeveloped countries. Also, agriculture continues to be a depressed sector as the production per person engaged in it is very low. Besides, dependence of agriculture on monsoon, outdated techniques of production, predominance of food crop in production, poverty of farmers, etc are the facts that speak of the backwardness of Indian agriculture.

Heavy Population Pressure

A high level of birth rate coupled by falling level of death rates. The fast rate of growth of population necessitates a higher rate of economic growth in order to maintain the same standard of living of the population. The rising population imposes greater economic burden – food, clothing, shelter, etc. Rising population leads to an increase in labour force. Increased labour force leads to unemployment.

Prevalence of Chronic Unemployment and Underemployment

It is difficult to provide gainful employment to the entire working population. In India, there exists 'distinguished employment' in agriculture. In rural areas, both unemployment and underemploy-ment exist side by side. So, urban employment and rural employment constitute an indivisible problem. Unemployment leads to wastage of manpower and the volume of production falls. Low rate of per capita income leads to low rate of savings. Low rate of savings means low rate of investment and low investment results in low production and which in turn results in low level of employment.

Low Rate of Capital Formation

Capital formation plays an important role in the economic development of a country. The amount of capital per head available and current rate of capital formation are low. The low ratio of capital formation causes low growth rate of national product. In the context of rising population, the present rate of capital formation, though high, is still not adequate. Presently, the level of investment has risen to about 24 per cent, as against 29 per cent in Japan, 26 per cent in Sweden and 24 per cent in Sri Lanka.

Mal-distribution of Wealth/Assets

There exist sharp inequalities in asset distribution between urban and rural households, therefore of which there is unequal distribution of income. Urban household indicates much worse asset distribution than rural household. According to the *World Development Report in India*, the poorest 10 per cent of population gets 3.5 per cent share in the national income, as against it the richest 100; 0 people enjoy 33.5 per cent of the national income. It may be noted that due to unequal distribution of wealth and income rich people of many countries like Japan, America, England, etc. had saved a large part of their income and used it to augment capital formation. However, rich Indians squander away their wealth in luxurious life-style.

Poor Quality of Human Capital

Country is suffering from mass illiteracy. Illiteracy retards growth. Capital means any resources; human capital includes expenditure on education, skill formation, research and improvements in health. When the standard of living of the labourers is low, they are ignorant and have poor health; their efficiency is bound to be low. It leads to high cost and poor quality of production. All this means low income of the labourers and they remain entrenched in the vicious circle of poverty.

Demographic Characteristics of an Underdeveloped Country

There is high density of population as the average expectation of life is low and infant mortality rates are high. A higher density imposes greater burden on land and other natural resources. The existence of a greater problem of the population in the lower age group is that it acts against production, but favours a higher level of consumption.

The Socio-economic Indicators of Consumption

On account of the low per capita income in India, the level of consumption of necessary things like food, clothing, shelter, etc., is also low. In India, a person gets in his food just 2.415 calories and 59 grams of protein. There is a failure to secure a balanced diet, low calorie intake and low level of consumption and protein because of which there is low level of living of an average Indian. Thus, because of low standard of living of the people, their productivity is also low. India is far behind the developed countries as far as standard of living and illiteracy is concerned.

Prevalence of Low Level of Technology

A majority of the productive units and a major part of output are produced with the help of techniques. New techniques are expensive and require a considerable degree of skill for their application in production. For new technology, we require availability of capital and training of an adequate number of personnel. In several Indian industries and in a very large sector of agriculture a low level of technology is being practised. Old and outdated machines are still in operation in industries like textile, sugar, etc. Production with such obsolete machinery not only adds to the cost but it is also of poor quality. The low level of technology causes low productivity and poor exploitation of resources.

Poor Economic and Social Organisation

The creation of a better institutional pattern of ownership is necessary to release the productive energies of people. All institutional bottlenecks require the development of an efficient and honest administration. In India, there is a great scarcity of skilled administrators, and the tradition of honest administration is lacking.

Many social institutions like the caste system, joint family system, laws of inheritance, customs, religious institutions, etc., serve as a stumbling block to economic development. Due to such an influence, people do not like to abandon their traditional way of doing things; rather they are averse to new methodology based on scientific principles. The result is that modern technology is not so readily adopted and thus the scarce resources of the country go waste.

Economic Planning in India

Among the underdeveloped democratic countries of the world, India was the first country that had chosen the path of planning for its development. Economic planning refers to that process wherein (i) a central planning authority (ii) keeping in view the resources of the country (iii) makes an attempt to control economic factors (iv) with a view to achieve pre-determined objectives within a specified period of time.

After independence, India had launched a programme of Five Year Plans to make the optimum use of country's available resources and remove its under development. Since the year 1951, a continuous process of Five-year plans has been going on.

Five-Year Plan	*Term of the Plan*	*Growth Rate*
First	1951-56	3.7
Second	1956-61	4.1
Third	1961-66	2.4
Three One-Year Plan	1966-69	3.7
Fourth	1969-74	3.3
Fifth	1974-79	5.0
Sixth	1979-85	5.4
Seventh	1985-90	5.7
Eighth	1992-97	6.6
Ninth	1997-2002	6.5
Tenth	2002-07	8.0
Eleventh	2008-2013	9.1

Figure 1: Five-Year Plans

The Planning Commission of 1950

After independence in 1950, the planning commission was set up under the chairmanship of the late Jawaharlal Nehru. It was to formulate plans for the economic development of the country on the basis of the available physical, capital and human resources. Within 15 months of its inception, it presented the draft of the first five-year plan to the government in July 1951. On 8 December 1952, Nehru presented the final draft of the first five-year plan to the Lok Sabha. The Prime Minister of India is the chairman of the planning commission.

Features of Planning

The main features of the developmental plans initiated in India are as follows:

1. Democratic

In India, economic planning has assumed a new pattern. It is democratic planning. In it, importance has been given to the development of both public and private sectors. To make planning a success, the operation of the people has been sought. But unlike the planning in socialist countries, in India neither the public nor the private sector is legally bound to achieve the targets of the plans. Indian planning is therefore aptly called Indicative Planning. In India, plans merely offer a future structure with regard to the direction of economic development, their objectives, their composition and the availability of financial resources for them. It is hoped that units of private and public sector will implement the plan in conformity with the structure. Government makes necessary provisions for its implementation. It provides incentives to the private sector and also controls it. However, to enforce the plans fully is not compulsory for either sector.

2. Different Sectors

Developmental plans in India are being executed by three sectors in consonance with mixed economy: (i) Public Sector (ii) Private Sector (iii) Joint Sector. Keeping in view the all-round development of the country, different tasks have been assigned to these sectors. The public sector plays a significant role in the development of basic industries and industries making defence equipment. The private sector has greater importance in the development of agriculture, small industries and industries producing mass consumption goods. Regarding the allocation of financial resources more importance is given to the public sector than the private sector in the plans.

3. Decentralised Decisionmaking

A comprehensive plan for the whole country is prepared by the planning commission in India. Subsequently, the planning board of each state makes a detailed plan of its own state. Some economic decisions by the private sector are taken in the light of price-mechanism. Before giving it a final shape, the plan is discussed and debated upon by the National Development Council and representatives of the people.

4. Financial Planning

Indian planning has grown as a financial planning. It means that more emphasis has been laid on the achievement of financial targets as against the physical targets. As a result of it, the total outlay in the third and fourth plans exceeded the targets, yet most of the physical targets could not be achieved. There has been considerable gap between physical targets and their actual achievements.

5. Unrealistic Data

In 1951 when the era planning began in India, reliable statistics were not available. The success of planning depends largely on dependable statistics. Although the position of statistics has improved a lot, yet it is far from satisfactory. It is one of the big drawbacks of our planning.

6. Broader Objective

The objectives of Indian planning are not only economic but social, cultural and political also. The objective of the plans is not restricted to economic growth alone but growth with justice.

7. Prospective and Perspective Planning

Indian planning is both prospective and perspective planning. In other words, both short-term and long-term programmes have been incorporated in five-year plans. It is so because without making short-term plans, a part of the long-term plans and real potentialities cannot be known. Thus, in the five-year plans, targets of employment and national income have to be determined on the basis of short term and long-term planning.

8. Planning by Inducement and Direction

Five year plans in India are mostly implemented by inducement, that is, after the blueprint of the plan is ready, people's co-operation to implement the same is sought. However, if needed, efforts are also made to enforce it by direction, keeping in view the larger interest of the country.

9. Comprehensive

The scope of our plans is very vast. Plans have been formulated in respect of different sectors of the economy, namely, agriculture, industry, communication transport, power, export, import, social services and optimum use of natural resources.

10. No Proper Implementation

Another feature of our planning is that the planning commission of India has paid more attention to the formulation of the plan. No serious thought has been given as to how these plans can be effectively and promptly implemented. Prof. Barbara Ward has rightly, said, "India's Planning has been stronger on formulation than on implementation."

Objectives of Planning

1. Increase in National Income or Economic Development

The objective of each plan in India to increase the national income or to accelerate the economic development. Increase in the national income helps economic development of the country. The objective of the first plan was to increase the national income of the country at the rate of 2.2 per cent per annum, but actually it increased at the rate of 3.7 per cent per annum at the 1993-94 prices. The second plan's objective was to raise the national income at the rate of 4.6 per cent per annum but it could increase only at the rate of 4.2 per cent per annum. The third plan aimed at raising the national income at the rate of 5 per cent per annum, but actual increase was 2.8 per cent per annum. The fourth plan's target was 5.5 per cent increase in national income per year but actually only 3 per cent increase could become possible. The fifth plan also set a target of 5.5 per cent increase in national income every year, but the actual realisation was 4.9 per cent. The sixth plan's target of 5.2 per cent growth rate was fully achieved. The seventh plan had set a target of 5 per cent increase in national income but actual realisation was 5.8 per cent. The objective of the eighth plan is to achieve a target of 5.6 per cent increase in the national income but the actual rate of growth was 6.5 per cent. The target of ninth plan was to achieve a growth rate of 6.5 per cent per annum. But the actual rate of growth was 5.5 per cent. The target of the ninth plan was to achieve a growth rate of 6.5 per cent per annum. But the actual rate of growth was 5.5 per cent.

The target of the tenth plan is to achieve a growth rate of 8 per cent.

2. Increase in Standard of Living

The other objective of the five-year plans was to raise the standard of living of the people so that their economic prosperity may grow. Improvement in the standard of living depends on several factors, like, high per capita income, price stability, equal distribution of income, etc.

3. To Reduce Economic Inequality

One of the main objectives of the five-year plans is to reduce economic inequality. Economic inequalities in the country symbolise exploitation and injustice. As a result, rich become richer and poor become poorer. In order to achieve economic equality, several measures were taken, viz., taxes were levied on the rich at progressive rates, public sector was expanded, and new licensing policy was adopted. The objective of Socialistic Pattern of Society was set during the second plan to achieve this aim.

4. Comprehensive Development

Five-year plans also aim at comprehensive development of the economy. In these plans, all-round development of all productive sectors like agriculture, industry, transport, trade, power, etc. has been envisaged. However, development of these sectors has not been uniform in each plan. During the first plan great stress was laid on the development of agriculture and irrigation, and in the second plan the main emphasis was on the development of heavy industries. In the fifth plan, development of both agriculture and industry was the sole objective, yet it was industrial development that received increasing attention. In the sixth and seventh plans development of power and energy was on the priority list.

5. Regional Development

Different parts of India are not uniformly developed from the economic point of view. Punjab, Haryana, Goa, Maharashtra, Gujarat, Tamil Nadu, Andhra Pradesh, etc. are relatively more developed economically whereas Bihar, Orissa, Nagaland, Meghalaya, Rajasthan, etc., are quite backward. One of the objectives of the five year plans is to attain regional equality by rapid development of backward states.

6. Economic Stability

In order to maintain the rate of economic growth, it is very essential to attain the goal of economic stability. Five year plans also aim at achieving economic stability. It implies an economy free from the alternating cycles of boom and depression. If prices rise very high or fall very low then the entire economy will be put out of gear. In every five year plan, one of the objectives has been economic stability in the country. As a result of economic development, some rise in prices is inevitable but it should not be excessive. Prices had started rising steeply from the very beginning of the seventh plan.

7. Self-sufficiency and Self-sustained Growth

The aim of the five-year plan is to render agricultural and industrial sectors self-sufficient in the light of the available resources. It has been one of the objectives of the plans to render the country self-sufficient in foodgrains, raw materials and such industry raw materials such as iron, steel, etc. To achieve this end, on the one hand imports are to be restricted producing import-substitutes in the country and on the other hand, exports are to be promoted. The objective of the plans is to attain self-sustained growth of the economy by raising the rate of saving and investment. After the third plan, the Indian economy has entered the 'take-off stage'. The plans aim at getting rid of dependence or foreign aid by promoting export trade and developing internal resources.

8. Social Justice

The objective of each plan in India is to promote social justice. It can be achieved in two ways. Firstly, by alleviating the poverty of the poorest of the poor. About 26 per cent of the population lives below the poverty line in India. To achieve it, the Minimum Needs Programme has been initiated. The other aspect of the social justice is to reduce economic inequality and have equal distribution of wealth and income.

9. Increase in Employment

Another objective of the plans is the optimum utilisation of manpower resources and increasing of employment opportunities. During planning period efforts have been made to provide employment to millions of people. In the seventh plan, great emphasis was laid on self-employment. More facilities were created for self-employment. In the eighth plan, maximum emphasis had been laid on the removal of unemployment and under-employment.

10. Increase in Investment and Saving

Each plan aims at increasing the ratio of investment in the national income. It augments the production capacity of the country. The rate of investment was to be increased to 8 per cent in the first plan, 12.7 per cent in the second plan, 14 in the third plan, 15.7 per cent in the fourth plan, 19.7 per cent in the fifth plan, 24.5 per cent in the sixth plan, 25.9 per cent in the seventh plan and 23.7 per cent in the eighth plan. To increase the rate of investment, it is necessary of increase the rate of saving and limit the rate of consumption. The rate of gross domestic saving in the seventh plan was 20.6 per cent. It reached 25 per cent of GDP in the eighth plan. The target of the ninth plan was to achieve 28.1 per cent growth rate of savings and 28.2 per cent growth rate of investment.

Hence, planning is aimed at utilising effectively physical and human resources, increasing the production of goods and services and reducing inequalities of wealth, income and opportunities.

Centralised and Decentralised Planning

Planning can be classified into:

1. *Centralisation:* Decisions are taken at the most senior or central level.

2. *Decentralisation:* Decisions are taken at some level lower than the most senior, typically by individual work units within the organisation or even by individual staff.
3. *Core-periphery:* Decisions are taken at both senior and lower levels, either separately or in an integrated manner.

After independence, India decided to have a planned economy of the Soviet model despite the fact that there was a difference of opinion among various economists on whether the model made centralised planning compulsory or there was scope for decentralisation. Centralised planning, as we all know, created lots of regional imbalances. Thus, the mineral-rich eastern states like Bihar and Orissa remained essentially backward because of lack of infrastructure and planned development. On the other hand, the states traditionally close to the centre like Punjab and Haryana, developed despite a lack of natural resources. The concept of decentralised planning can be traced back to the pre-independence days and the philosophy of Mahatma Gandhi who was an ardent advocate of small village-based communities that would be more or less self-sufficient.

Decentralisation is defined as, "an even distribution of power (in any or all of many forms) among all agents in the social, political and economic spheres." Decentralisation governance, from state capitals to towns and villages, helps to facilitate participation in the country's development by people from all socio-economic strata.

The top to bottom model envisages a situation where the powers enjoyed by the people lower down the hierarchy are at the pleasure of the higher-ups. In fact, it is the class at the top of the pyramid that should be held to the grassroots level support for its privileges. Decentralisation is both vertical and horizontal. The horizontal decentralisation distributes power among institutions at the same level, while vertical decentralisation envisages delegation of power by the higher authority to the lower ones.

Therefore, planning in India has the following three characteristics:

1. The process operates under a democratic framework with elected government at the centre and the states.

2. The planning process operates through a system of federation where concurrent planning is involved.
3. The planning process operates in a market-friendly economy.

A critical review of India's experience with development planning and its interface is the evolving mode of production and strategy of development. Development planning in India raises a number of central, methodological and institutional questions related to the planning process.

2

Public Sector in Economic Development

The public sector includes all those industrial and commercial enterprises that are owned and funded by the government to manage them on its behalf. The public sector covers all government departments, government enterprises, railways, communication, irrigation projects, ordinance factories, banking and insurance companies, public financials, institutes, government schools, colleges, hospitals, dispensaries, etc. Taking into account the economic analysis, we focus our attention only on the industrial and commercial enterprises of the government.

The Evolution of the Public Sector in India

Prior to 1947, there was virtually no "public sector" in the Indian economy. The only instances worthy of mention were the railways, the posts and the telegraphs, the port trusts, the ordnance and aircraft factories and a few state-managed undertakings like the government salt factories, quinine factories, etc. The idea that economic development should be promoted by the state actually managing industrial concerns did not take root in India before 1947.

However, in the post-independence period, the expansion of public sector was undertaken as an integral part of the 1956 industrial policy.

The industrial policy resolution 1956 gave the public sector a strategic role in the Indian economy. For one thing, at the time of independence, the country was backward and under-developed— basically an agrarian economy with a weak industrial base, heavy unemployment, low level of savings and investment and near absence of infrastructural facilities due to which Indian economy needed a big push.

The Industrial Policy 1991 provides an approach to public enterprises. The new policy emphasized that the measures must be taken to make these enterprises more growth-oriented and technically dynamic. According to new industrial policy, the priority areas for growth of public enterprise in the future will be the following:

1. Essential infrastructure goods and services
2. Exploration and exploitation of oil and mineral resources.
3. Technology development and building of manufacturing capabilities in areas that are crucial in the long – term development of the economy and where private sector is inadequate.
4. Manufacture of products where strategic considerations predominate such as defence equipment.

Government will strengthen those public enterprises that fall in the reserved areas of operation or are in high priority areas or are generating good or reasonable profits. Such enterprises will be provided a much greater degree of management autonomy through the system of memorandum of understanding.

Competition will also be induced in these areas for private sector participation. In case of selected enterprises, part of government holdings in the equity share capital of these enterprises will be disinvested. In order to provide further market discipline to the performance of public enterprises, various measures such as common detriment, control of monopolies and prohibition of monopolistic and restrictive and unfair trade practices were taken.

The portfolio of public sector investments will be reviewed with a view to focus the public sector on strategic, high tech and essential infrastructure, whereas some reservation for areas of exclusivity to be opened up to the private sector selectively.

Public sector companies which are chronically sick and which are unlikely to be turned out well, for the formulation of revival/ rehabilitation schemes, be referred to the Board for Industrial and

Financial Reconstruction (BIFR) or other similar high level institutions created to protect the interest of the workers likely to be affected by such rehabilitation packages.

In order to raise resources and encourage wider public participation a part of government shareholding in the public sector would be offered to mutual funds, financial institutions, general public and workers. Boards of public sector companies would be made more professional and given greater powers.

There will be a greater thrust on performance improvement through the memorandum of understanding (MOU) system through which managements would be the part of it. The government would be upgraded to make MOU negotiations and their implementations more effective.

Public Enterprise Policy

The governments strategy towards the public sector, continues to encompass a judicious mix of strengthening strategic units, privatising non-strategic ones through gradual disinvestments or strategic sale and devising viable rehabilitation strategic for weak units.

The main elements of government policy towards public sector units are:

a) Bring down government equity in all non-strategic public sector units to 26 per cent or lower, if necessary.
b) Reconstruction and revive potentially viable public sector units.
c) Close down public sector units which cannot be revived.
d) Fully protect the interest of workers.

To make public sector enterprises more efficient and competitive, the government has granted autonomy, of varying degrees, to selected profit making public sector enterprises. Depending upon the degree of autonomy granted, the select industries are called Navratnas and Mini-ratnas.

Navratnas

The government has selected 11 public enterprises for the Navratnas category. These enterprises, subject to certain guidelines, have full freedom to make capital Expenditure decision regarding joint ventures and setting up of subsidiary offices abroad for technology and strategic alliance.

Mini-Ratnas

Government has also granted enhanced financial, managerial and operational autonomy to other profit-making enterprises, called mini-ratnas. These enterprises should have earned profits continuously for last three years, have positive net worth, do not seek budgetary support or guarantees from the government and have not defaulted in the repayment of loans/ interests to the government. These enterprises can incur capital expenditure, enter into joint ventures, set up technological and strategic alliances, formulate schemes of HRM, etc., subject to certain stipulations and guidelines.

Objectives of Public Sector in India

1. To Ensure Rapid Economic Development

State could gather the necessary resources and make direct investment in various sectors of the economy, and thus increase the speed of industrial and economic development. It could create the necessary infrastructure for development by making investment in power, transport, and irrigation sector and accelerate the development process.

2. To Promote Redistribution of Income and Wealth

It was necessary that concentration of income, wealth and economic power in the hands of a few rich capitalists be curbed. The public sector's expansion was regarded as the best way to do that. In industrial enterprises which are owned and managed by the government, profits do not go to the capitalists but accrue to the government; reinvest them in industry or spend them on other social welfare programmes.

3. To Develop Industries that Require Huge Investments

There are some industries the development of which is absolutely essential for growth of economy. Industries like power, transport, petroleum, fertilisers, iron and steel, heavy machinery needs attention for economic growth. Industries require such large investments that may be beyond the means of private entrepreneurs.

4. To Achieve Balanced Regional Growth

Expansion of public sector was necessary to industrialise the backward regions and achieve a balanced regional growth. Since, backward regions lack facilities for industrial growth, such as they are short of power, transport, labour training facilities, or are far away from the sources of raw materials, or markets, the private entrepreneur would naturally not like to risk his investment there.

5. To Prevent Concentration of Economic Power

When more and more industries pass on into hands of a few private industrial houses, this is called concentration of economic power. This may allow private enterprises to dominate the industrial scenario as they can control the volume of output and manipulate market prices. This is clearly detrimental to the welfare of the consumers and against the interest of the society. To prevent such concentration of economic power, it was though necessary to establish public enterprises, offer competition to the private sector.

6. To Generate Resources of Development

Public enterprises were expected to generate sufficient surpluses (profits) that would be ploughed back to set up more public enterprises or used for the expansion of the existing enterprises.

7. To Promote Import Substitution

Public sector industries were expected to produce goods of international standards so as to replace the imported goods. Since, the country did not have plenty of foreign exchange to import equipments as well as some consumer goods, it was expected that public sector would produce and provide goods as a replacement or a substitute for imported goods.

8. To Generate Employment

The public sector was expected to generate substantial employment opportunities and help in minimising the dimensions and problems of widespread unemployment.

9. To Help in Development of Small-scale Industries

The public sector was also expected to help the growth of small–scale industries by enabling them to upgrade their technology and including them to produce ancillary products (parts) required as inputs by these enterprises.

10. To Assume Commanding Heights of the Economy

Commanding heights refer to a position from where the government can decide and make necessary changes and thus direct the economy towards attainment of desired objectives. Through the development of public enterprises in all the key sectors, the government would come to assume 'the commanding heights' of the economy and would thus be in a position to dilute such tendencies of concentration of economic power in private hands and blunt their capacity to exploit the consumers or hold the economy to ransom.

Role of Public sector

1. Infrastructure Development by the Public Sector

Development of basic and capital goods industries and creation of infrastructure involve heavy investment, low yield and long gestation period. These investments were, therefore, not attractive to the private sector as it could not raise such huge resources. Naturally, it was left to the government to develop them, and most of the public enterprises were set up in these industries.

2. Strong Industrial Base in India

Despite many criticisms against the public sector enterprises, there is no denying the fact that rapid industrialisation in the first three decades after independence was mainly due to the public sector. The industrial policy resolutions reserved certain industries – atomic energy, ammunition and armaments, aircrafts, etc.—with the government in the interest of national security.

Government had come in a big way to undertake the development of basic and strategic industries, capital goods industries and even some consumer goods industries. A strong industrial base has been laid, though there are still many weaknesses and gaps in the industrial structure of the country. Credit has to be given to the public sector for this achievement. Even after the introduction of economic reforms, the private sector investment has not increased as expected and it is being suggested that the public sector should take up the responsibility of infrastructure development.

3. Dominance of Public Sector in Critical Areas

In highly critical areas such as copper, lead, coal, petroleum products, hydro and steam turbines the share of public sector is 100 per cent. In quite a large number of products, it ranges between 50 and 95 per cent.

4. Role of Public Sector in Export Promotion

Most of the public sector enterprises have been started keeping in mind the requirements of the Indian economy in the fields of production and distribution. However, some public enterprises have done much to promote India's exports. The State Trading Corporation (STC) and the Minerals and Metals Trading Corporation (MMTC) have done a wonderful job of export promotion in all parts of the world, especially in the East European countries. The metal ores have become the second largest single item on our list of exports has been due to pioneering efforts of these organisations. Considerable success has been achieved in pushing up the exports of Indian handicrafts, light engineering goods and many other new items of exports. The

Hindustan Steel Ltd, the Bharat Electronics Ltd, the Hindustan Machine Tools, etc., are some of the public sector enterprises that are exporting increasing proportion of output and earning foreign exchange.

5. Role of the Public Sector in Import Substitution

Entry of Hindustan Antibiotics Ltd. and the Indian Drugs and Pharmaceuticals Ltd. (IDPL) into the manufacture of drugs and pharmaceuticals so as to remove the monopolistic stranglehold of foreign concerns in this field helped India save foreign exchange used for importing these items. Likewise, the Oil and Natural Gas Commission (ONGC) and the Indian Oil Corporation Ltd. (IOC) are public enterprises that attempt directly to increase self-reliance of the country and reduce our dependence on imports. Complete self-sufficiency may not be possible at present, but a determined effort should be made to achieve this goal in the shortest possible time.

6. Role of Public Sector in Raising Internal Resources

Internal resources consist of depreciation and retained profits. With every five-year plan, the public sector was able to mobilise larger internal resources. During the eighth plan, PSUs generated internal resources to the order of Rs.1,01,212 crores—a creditable record indeed. During 1998-99, internal resources generation was to the order of Rs. 31,300 crores. It is really encouraging to note that central public enterprises have succeeded in increasing their internal resource generation over the years. This trend should be welcomed.

7. Contribution to the Exchequer

Apart from generation of internal resources and payment of dividend, public enterprises have been making substantial contribution to the government exchequer through payment of corporate taxes, excise duty, customs duty and other duties; in this way they help in mobilising funds for financing the needs for the planned development of the country.

Causes for the Expansion of Public Enterprises

In a developing economy like India, nationalising some of the industrial, banking and insurance units and starting new units was essential to help in speeding up the rate of growth. Therefore, public enterprises became an essential part of the economic development programme of India.

1. Rate of Economic Development and Public Enterprises

The public sector was essential to realise the target of the high rate of development deliberately fixed by the government. To fulfil this ambitious plan target, the government had to resort to compulsory saving through taxation. The government and other important policy-making bodies like the planning commission are under the normal human temptation to use the funds under the government's own aegis. Also, the government has to keep constant check and balance if they provide funds to private sector enterprises for industrial development, resulting in unnecessary botheration.

2. Pattern of Resources Allocation and Public Enterprises

In professor Ramanadham's words "the main reason for the expansion of the public sector lies in the pattern of resources allocation decided upon under the plans." For instance, in the second plan the emphasis was shifted to industries and mining, mainly basic and capital goods industries to be developed under the aegis of the public sector. Thus, more resources for industrialisation were funneled through the public sector. Under these circumstances, "it is inevitable that the public sector must grow not only absolutely but also relatively to the private sector."

3. Removal of Regional Disparities through Public Enterprises

Another important reason for the extension of the public sector was the anxiety for balanced development in different parts of the country and to see that there were no serious regional disparities. Good examples are the setting up of the three steel plants at Bhilai, Rourkela and Durgapur and the Neyveli project in Madras that were meant to help industrialise the regions surrounding the projects. Without central government assistance growth in such areas had just been a disclaim.

4. Sources of Funds for Economic Development

Surplus of government enterprises could be re-invested in the same industries or used for the establishment and expansion of other industries. Industries can also plough back whole or substantial amount of their profits for expansion. However, profits in private enterprises are declared as dividends among shareholders. This would only create inequalities among people. But profits of the public sector industries can be directly used for capital formation.

5. Socialistic Pattern of Society

The socialistic pattern of society calls for extension of the public sector. We may quote the second five-year plan here." The adoption of the socialistic pattern of society as the national objective, as well as the need for planned and rapid development require that all industries of basic and strategic importance, or in the nature of public utility services should be in the public sector. Other industries which are essential and require investment on a scale which only the state, in present circumstances, could provide, have also to be in the public sector." Public enterprises were used as major instruments for the reduction of inequalities of income and to bring about a more equitable distribution of income in several ways; (a) The profits of public enterprises would go directly to the government. (b) There could be effective regulation of income of top executives in public enterprises (c) The public enterprises could be asked to adopt discriminatory price policies which would benefit the low-income consumers (d) It is easy to raise wage income of the low paid staff. Extension of the public sector enterprise will be followed by a substantial growth in the volume of national saving and investment as well as the funds available for government outlay on social services; without public enterprise, there can be no private enterprise. In fact, it is the former that enables the full growth of the latter.

6. Limitation and Abuses of the Private Sector

The behaviour and attitude of the private sector itself was an important factor responsible for the expansion of the public sector in the country. Certain sectors in which private sector wanted to move did not had the necessary resources. This was understandable but the private sector was unwilling to take even the normal risks of business. During the second plan period and later, many of the licences issued to the private sector for setting up fertiliser units were surrendered when the need for fertiliser production was paramount for the country to push an agricultural breakthrough. In a number of cases, the government was forced to take over a private sector industry or industrial units either in the interest of workers or to prevent excessive exploitation of consumers. The private sector life insurance companies were taken over by the government to protect the interest of the insured from the short-sighted and rapacious private exploiters. The top 20 commercial banks were nationalised, among other things, to prevent bank funds being used for building up private industrial and commercial empires. The take over of sick cotton mills was due to the failure of the private sector. The point to note here is that often, the private sector did not function as it should and did not carry out its social responsibilities. Accordingly, the government was forced to take over or nationalise the private sector units.

The expansion of the public sector was aimed at the fulfilment of our national goals, viz., the removal of poverty, the attainment of self-reliance, reduction in inequalities of income, expansion of employment opportunities, removal of regional imbalances, acceleration of the pace of agricultural and industrial development, to reduce concentration of ownership and prevent growth of monopolistic tendencies by acting as effective counterveiling power to the private sector, to make the country self-reliant in modern technological and managerial cadres so as to ultimately rid the country from dependence on foreign resources.

PERFORMANCE OF PUBLIC SECTOR UNDERTAKINGS

While the government has been pushing ahead with more and more public sector undertakings, there has been considerable criticism about the poor performance and in some cases utter failure of government undertakings in the country. Some economists have argued that profit should not be used as a criterion for judging the performance of public enterprises instead they should be guided by a variety of considerations in determining prices, and it would not be appropriate to use profit as one of the criterion of their efficiency. This is particularly so in social utility services, like railways, posts and telegraphs, supply of water, electric energy, etc. The state should not raise the prices of these services, even though costs may have risen. Similarly, the public enterprises have a bulk of their investment in heavy and basic enterprises. Such enterprises have long gestation period and a part of the investment may be under construction. It would, therefore, be appropriate to calculate the rate of return on effective capital employed and thus not include the capital employed of undertakings under construction or in expansion or capital work-in-progress. In other words, "profitability" of the running concerns alone should not be the index of their performance. Moreover, PSUs offer much better reward for labour in terms of wages and salaries and other perquisites in comparison with small and medium enterprises in the private sector. To judge their performance, an adjustment should, therefore, be made for a higher social rate of return. Although profit maximisation (or in the case of public enterprises, the generation of surplus) may not be the sole criterion to judge their performance, yet it cannot be denied that it would be a folly to ignore it altogether. Thus the principle of profit maximisation has a negative virtue as it impels enterprises to reduce waste of resources and inefficiency arising there from.

Shortcomings of the Public Sector

There is much scope for improving the efficiency and working of public sector enterprises:

1. Mounting Losses

A review of the working of public sector enterprises reveals that either the profits in them have been deplorably low or that they have been making losses. The biggest losses are made by SEBs

(State Electricity Boards). It is estimated that the losses incurred by SEBs on their sale of power to agricultural and domestic sector rose from Rs.7,450 crores in 1991-92 to Rs.19,230 crores in 1996-97. These losses were incurred because power was supplied at a mere 18 paise per unit as against the production and distribution cost of Rs. 1.53 per unit. It is the losses of the central government enterprises, which have generally received maximum publicity. The worst culprits in this respect are to be found among state governments. The state electricity boards, the irrigation works, the road transport corporations and other state government owned enterprises have the most scandalous record of making losses. The government should, therefore, make a case-by-case study of the loss incurring enterprises and take remedial action.

2. Political Factors Influence Decision about Location

Powerful ministers in the ruling party make promises about the future location of projects in a state irrespective of the results of the feasibility study about costs. This approach leads to a considerable wastage of capital resources.

Example: A classic instance of this political and irrational approach is the decision of the central government to break-up the MIG aircraft project into two parts to be located in two separate states. These two locations – Nasik and Korakut – are over 900 kms apart. This was done to satisfy two powerful political bosses from two states.

3. Delay in Completion and Increase in Costs of Construction

Many of the projects took longer time to complete than was initially envisaged. For instance, in the case of Trombay fertilisers project, it took six to seven years to complete. The original estimate of cost was Rs. 27 crores (1959) and the final cost stood at about Rs. 40 crores (1965). It is very necessary to prepare comprehensive construction plans so that the avoidable delays and increases in costs should not put additional burden on the scarce resources.

4. Over-capitalisation

Public sector projects are charged with over-capitalisation. In other words, the input-output ratio obtaining in many projects was unfavourable. "The causes leading to over-capitalisation can be traced to inadequate planning, delays and avoidable expenditure during construction, surplus machine capacity, tied aid resulting in the compulsion to purchase imported equipment on a non-competitive basis, expensive turn key contracts, bad location of projects and the provision of housing and other amenities on a liberal scale."

5. Price Policy

It would be suicidal from the point of view of the overall growth of the economy if the prices of steel, oil, fertilisers or coal were fixed very high. The public sector has to keep in mind the social implications of its price policy. In this connection, it is important to remember that in many cases, under the public pressure, prices are kept low even when costs and prices have been rising. This naturally affects commercial profitability. Pricing policies are not rational. They have no declared price policy, except perhaps that they have some departmental directives and ad hoc piecemeal orders. It is being gradually realised in the country that profit should be recognised as an index of efficiency and that the profit motive is not inconsistent with the broad objective of the socialist pattern of society.

6. Use of Man–power Resources in Excess of Actual Requirements

There is poor manpower planning and this is clearly reflected in the inadequate arrangements for training and education of workers. The unsatisfactory salary and wage rates and the absence of incentives to staff have resulted in the flight of personnel from the public sector to the private sector. It has been suggested that top position in a public sector undertaking should also be opened to its employees. Labour indiscipline was one of the causes for the poor performance of the public sector enterprises in recent years. Indiscipline among the workers and poor management plagued many of the large government enterprises. Supervision is also difficult in giant undertakings. The situation is not very healthy; government should make a determined bid to improve industrial relations.

7. Capacity Utilisation

This is certainly not an optimum situation. It is very necessary to find the causes of low capacity utilisation and thus remedy the situation by appropriate measures.

8. Faulty Controls

The poor performance of public sector enterprises is often ascribed to faulty controls, financial and otherwise, exercised over them. At present, the finance ministry and the minister-in-charge of the undertaking and the parliament exercises control. Parliamentary control over the operations and capital development plans of public enterprises tend to become quite rigid. There is, therefore, the need to provide greater functional autonomy to the management of public enterprises.

9. Inefficient Management

For efficiency in business and industrial enterprises it is necessary that operational decisions are prompt. This necessitates a large measure of autonomy and flexibility of operations in the government enterprises. Again, delegation of authority and elasticity in working are needed in a high degree. Unfortunately, there has been general failure to define responsibilities and duties in public sector enterprises in India. Finally, the successful operation of public enterprises is dependent upon the availability of experienced persons to fill up top positions. Public enterprises are sarcastically referred to as 'colonies for bureaucrats'. The government should progressively shift to professionalised management in these enterprises.

10. Higher Capital Intensities Leading to Lower-employment Generation

Since a large number of public enterprises were directed basic and heavy industries, they have shown higher capital intensities. In context of few new priorities of development which emphasize generation of employment and encouragement to small-scale industries, there is a need to re-orient policies and identify, within the existing group of industries, areas where less capital- intensive operations can be adopted without sacrificing quality and quantity of production. The present situation calls for a departure from the earlier approach in favour of a judicious selection of equipment, technologies and materials, which help to absorb manpower.

3

Privatisation and Disinvestment in India

Meaning and Concept

Privatisation refers to the dilution of government's stock that leads to effective change to the management and control. Privatisation is often seen as an ideologically-based programme, devised and driven by a powerful leader, motivated by a combination of intellectual conviction of benefits of free markets and hatred of power of organised labour. This was the start of most radical experiments in public policy, with major consequences in Britain and around the world. Privatisation is the process of transferring property from public ownership to private ownership or transferring of services, activities, operation and management from government to the private sector. The process of privatisation in India began in 1991-92 with the sale of the minority stakes in public sector units.

But one problem was that with the transfer of management into private hands, the interest of employees might suffer. The main motive of privatisation is to put national resources and assets to optimal use and in particular to unleash the productive potential of public sector units.

The policy of privatisation is aimed at:

1. Modernisation and upgradation of public sector enterprises
2. Creation of new assets
3. Generation of employment
4. Retiring of public debt
5. Setting up of disinvestments proceed fund.

Capitalists favours privatisation whereas socialists are against privatisation.

Advantages of Privatisation

1. Competition and Efficiency

It is argued that one major reason for inefficiency in the public sector is that most of the public enterprises do not face any competition in the market as they are mostly of a monopolistic nature, operating in a protected market. With privatisation of the public sector units, they will have to face severe competition from many other units that may springup, as the industrial sector is thrown open for the private players. This growing competition will compel the operating industrial units to make all kinds of improvements in their organisation, management and other associated operations to keep standing in the market. Thus, privatisation would ensure efficiency and would contribute to rapid industrial development of the economy.

2. Less Wastage and Reduced Costs

Since, private enterprise is based on the essential principle of profit maximisation, the privatisation of public sector enterprises would have to make all out-efforts to reduce costs by minimising wastages and adopting cost-saving techniques. Public sector enterprises are hardly bothered about their escalating costs because they are not held accountable for low profits or heavy losses. There is no efficiency audit and not many cost-saving measures are efficiently implemented. Thus, the high cost, high loss or low profit economy of the public sector needs to be replaced, in the national economic interest, by the low cost, high efficiency and profit maximising economic principles.

3. Better Use of Scarce Capital

The public sector, which has come to be associated with wastages, inefficiency, unprofessional management, etc., is not only a drain on the governments finances, it is also accused of wastefully using the country's most scarce resources, viz., capital. This is reflected by the ever-rising capital output ratio that increased from less than 2.0 in the first plan to over 6.6 in sixth plan and was nearly 4.9 by the end of 1995-96. The capital output ratio indicates how much capital is used (in value terms) to produce one unit of output. No doubt, some industries may have high capital output ratio due to their capital-intensive nature (such as steel industry). But an overall rise in this ratio from one plan to another only shows that the capital resources are being inefficiently used either due to their underutilisation or due to mishandling, mismanagement or due to inappropriate combination with other inputs and use of inefficient work practices.

4. Economy in Government Expenditure

The government of India provides subsidies on many commodities produced by the public sector enterprises so as to make their price affordable to common people. Thus, for example, government supplies highly subsidised fertilisers, pesticides, etc., to the farmers. Now, as most of these goods are produced by the high-cost public enterprises the amount subsidies continues to prevail at high levels. If these industries are privatised and consequent efficiency improvements result in bringing down the cost of production substantially, there will be no need for subsidies as the market prices would be lower.

5. Reduction in Budget Deficits

The public enterprises that continue to incur losses year after year are a great drain on the nation's resources. The loss of public sector units is an expenditure burden on the government's revenues. Further, the burden of subsidy on goods also adds to government expenditure. This gives rise to the budgetary deficits that are, in turn, financed by printing more money of deficit financing, thus causing inflation in the country.

6. Greater Investment, Larger Output and More Employment

Since the private sector is associated with efficient management and least wasteful operations, it can create both domestic as well as foreign surplus. As low cost high quality goods produced by the competitive private sector create their place in the national and international markets, the higher demand and profitability prospects draw more investment and this supports the expansion of the industrial and service sectors.

7. Flexibility in Decisionmaking

Timely and quick decisions are the essence of successful business. In the case of public sector, the decisionsmaking process is still centralised with the government and the various agencies involved in this process suffer from red tape and time-consuming procedures. Hence, the decisions are neither quick nor timely. And in case of any discrepancy in decisionmaking, the same long route may have to be followed for this. The private enterprises with their delegated authority and command structure are known for their quick decisionmaking and flexible policies that ensure best possible results.

8. Market Orientation of Production

The private sector works according to the market signals of what to produce and how much to produce. Since the objective of the private sector is to minimise profits, it would produce only those goods that sell well and ensure maximum returns. Thus, there will be no waste and no mismatch between what people demand and what industry produces.

9. No Justification of Public Sector in Purely Trading or Non-strategic Business

In our country, the public sector had expanded its activities to cover trading, financial and non-strategic activities like running departmental stores, flour mills, textile units, hotels, restaurants, etc. It is, therefore, necessary that the public sector should focus on as few as possible activities of strategic significance and leave the rest to the private sector.

Disadvantages of Privatisation

1. Privatisation Ignores Social Welfare

One of the major arguments in favour of the public sector has been that it works for promoting social welfare. On the other hand, the private sector operates with the objective of maximising private profits. For example, many goods of public use, whose production and prices were so regulated by the government as to be within the reach of the common people, have now become unaffordable for the poor after privatisation and decontrol of those industries.

2. Centralisation of Economic Power

Operation of the private sector is feared to lead to concentration of economic power in the hand of a few top capitalist entrepreneurs. This happens because market competition has a tendency to be unstable; either some big companies drive out the smaller one through constant price called 'cut-throat competition' or acquire the other companies through mergers and acquisitions. Such economic concentration can be harmful not only for the consumers, but may also lead to dominance of the few big companies over the country's political system and economic policies.

3. Privatisation may Lead to Unemployment and Poverty

Privatisation, which is associated with higher efficiency and quicker development, may in fact result it larger unemployment and greater poverty. This may happen because in their pursuit of cost reduction and higher profitability, the private entrepreneurs use the modern automatic production techniques that are highly capital intensive and use much smaller number of workers while the public sector pursues the objective of creating more employment as a social welfare measure.

4. Private Sector is not Always and Invariably all that Efficient and Enterprising

The case for privatisation of the public sector industrial and commercial units rests on the assumption that whereas all public sector units are inefficient and wasteful, the private sector enterprises are very efficient and helpful in faster economic development. However, the facts is that all the public sector units are not inefficient. There are public sector enterprises like the ONGC that are rated among the top companies in the world. The petroleum sector as a whole has performed quite satisfactorily. Thus, all public sector units need not be privatised. If possible, they should be reformed and remodelled.

Conclusion

Privatisation does not necessarily benefit the enterprises in terms of immediate accrual of resources. The proceeds of privatisation go towards the government. The extent of eventual privatisation in a particular PSU will depend on the classification of a PSU as strategic, core and non–core. Since the public sector units were set up with objectives relevant at different times, it has become necessary to review whether their continuation in the public sector is justified at present.

Disinvestment Policy

Disinvestment simply means diluting the stock of the government's stake in a public enterprise. The extent of disinvestment or dilution of the government's stake determines whether the control and management of the enterprise remains with the government or goes into the hands of the private shareholders. Thus, if the government sells 51 per cent or more shares of a public enterprise to the private shareholders, then this dilution of the government's stock involves transfer of management and control as well. In this case, the public sector unit can be said to have been privatised. But if the government offloads a small part of its stake, i.e., sells less than 50 per cent stock to the private shareholders then effective control of the enterprise still remains with the government. In this case, disinvestment has taken place, but not the privatisation. Thus, disinvestment is a wider term; it covers all dilutions of the government's stake whether it is accompanied by change in control or otherwise.

Disinvestment in India

In India, the public sector was established, carefully nurtured and strengthened to achieve the lofty ideals of a socialistic society that would be free from economic concentration and private exploitation, and would make rapid strides in the direction of economic development with social justice. It was designed to be the means of achieving of socialism and thus ushering in a social pattern that would be just and equitable. However, instead of providing resources for further development and becoming a symbol of social change, the public sector became synonymous with inefficiency, incompetence, red tapism and an instrument of political favouritism. It became a drag on the government's finances and a significant contributor to mounting fiscal deficits. Thus, something is needed to be done urgently to reform, rejuvenate and reorient this bulging sector.

Disinvestment in the public sector has thus been resorted to for two major reasons:

1. *To provide fiscal support to the government:* The objective of fiscal support is indeed weighty because of the compelling needs and demand of providing health, education and other social infrastructure that a developing society makes on the government. Financial resources are hard to come from other revenue sources and, thus, disinvestment can provide the required funds for use in these spheres. Receipts from disinvestment can also be used for retiring public debt and thus reducing the burden of interest payments that have acquired massive dimensions.
2. *To improve efficiency of public enterprises by introducing an element of accountability to the private shareholders:* The second important objective of disinvestment is to bring about improvement in efficiency in the working of these enterprises. No one can dispute the high degree of efficiency of a private enterprise, and thus, if disinvestment is large enough to transfer management control along with ownership to the private sector, efficiency levels are bound to improve. Even in cases where the extent of disinvestment is small and control still remains with the government, the induction of private ownership even on a part of stock of these enterprises can lead to efficiency gains, as accountability to private shareholders is bound to

have a salutary effect on the functioning of an enterprise. This is because the private shareholders would compel the management to run the enterprise more efficiently and profitably to provide them adequate return on their investment.

Mode of Disinvestment

The extent of disinvestment, i.e., how much of its stake the government should offload, is a policy decision, which the government has to take in conformity with the overall economic policy. Should the government sell its entire stake and privatise the industrial units or retain some control over management through lower doses of disinvestment, is an industrial policy decision which the government must take in accordance with what level of public/private ownership it considers healthy for the economy. Of course, there is a consensus that no disinvestment can be done in the strategic industries, e.g., atomic energy, national defence, railway, transport, etc. For non-strategic and non-core sectors, disinvestment can be done up to 51 per cent and beyond. For the rest of the enterprises, the criterion for disinvestment can be the extent of efficiency that could be brought about as well as the need to meet the financial requirements of the government.

About the mode of disinvestment, there are two acceptable and transparent processes available:

1. Offering for sale in the market, equity shares of the public enterprises at fixed prices, and
2. Sale of block equity (big block of shares) through auction to a predecided clientele.

In India, the government has followed both these methods. In case of many enterprises, disinvestment was done through the sale of the government's equity in the share market. Later, in many other cases, the bulk stock was sold through auctions to predetermined group of buyers, including the Tatas, Ambanis, etc.

There is a general criticism that disinvestment is like selling family silver (family assets), which should not have been done as a normal policy for raising revenues, but could be resorted to only in exceptional and emergent circumstances when urgently needed financial resources are not available through the normal channels. However, some economists do not subscribe to this view.

Resources raised through disinvestment should not be used for revenue expenditure, i.e., meeting day-to-day expenses of the government. They must be used either for creating new community assets, expanding social and economic services repaying public debt. A part of disinvestment process, say 10 per cent, as recommended by the Committee on Disinvestment, must be given to the enterprises themselves for their own expansion and financial strength.

Disinvestment Policy and Practice

The disinvestment process in India began in 1991-92 when the government sold shares of some public enterprises from its holding for Rs. 3,038 crores. This disinvestment was, however, in the nature of sale of 'minority shares', which means the government sold less than half the stock held by it in these enterprises so that it could retain their management control. Such minority share sale continued till 1999-2000, and during this period, the government realised Rs. 18,638 crores through this method of sale of shares.

However, this policy was changed in 2000-01 with the establishment of the Department of Disinvestment, which later was converted into the Ministry of Disinvestment. The new policy was to go in for strategic sale of the identified public sector undertakings. And thus in accordance with this decision, all disinvestment since the year 2000 has been in the form of strategic sales. Strategic sale is defined as a sale of equity by the government where the management control of the entity is handed over to the strategic partner. Typically, the strategic partner is required to purchase an equity stake, which is large enough to ensure a workable majority. Among the strategic sales under the disinvestment policy, some important companies where government's stake was sold are 18 ITDC hotels, VSNL, lOC, BPCL, GAIL, Maruti Udyog, etc.

Disinvestment in public enterprises is the only way to reduce the financial burden of public enterprises on the government. It is also expected to improve the efficiency of those enterprises with the availability of professional guidance from the private sector that gets involved as a partner in their progress. But the critics feel that by this policy of disinvestment the government is fulfilling the social responsibility of establishing a more equitable social system. To them, disinvestment is a clear move towards privatisation that would result in establishing a free economy and capitalist society with all its accompanying evils such as inequalities in income, wealth and concentration of economic power. But after having suffered the public sector for almost half a century it is now the time to go in for some drastic reforms, and disinvestment is the decision in the right direction.

One of the major concerns expressed with respect to privatisation is that with transfer of management into private hands, the interest of employees might suffer. Thus, provisions are made in the sale agreements that ensure that there is no retrenchment of employees at least for a period of one year after privatisation, and even after that, retrenchment is possible only under Voluntary Retirement Scheme (VRS). Provisions are also included to enhance the employee's welfare.

UPA Government's Policy on Disinvestment

The disinvestment process that began in 1991-92 with the sale of minority stakes in some public sector undertakings, shifted focus to strategic sales from the year 1999-2000 onwards. This process of strategic sales came in for some sharp critical comments from the opposition parties and even some well-known economists and social activists. Doubts have been raised about the proper valuation of assets before selling the PSUs, and whether the sale price, the persons and organisations to whom such strategic sales were made have gone through a transparent procedure.

According to the disinvestment policy of the new (UPA) government, all privatisations will be considered on a transparent procedure based on consultations and taken up on a case-by-case basis. The government would retain the existing 'navratna' companies in the public sector though these companies will be encouraged to raise resources from the capital market.

The UPA government is committed to a strong and effective public sector that will be geared to meet its social objectives while functioning on commercial lines. The government would devolve full managerial and commercial autonomy to successful profit making companies operating in a competitive environment. Generally, profit making public sector companies will not be privatised.

While every effort will be made to modernise and restructure sick public sector companies with a view to reviving them and making them economically viable, the chronically loss-making companies will, however, either be sold off or closed, after all workers get their legitimate dues and compensation. The government will take the help of private industry to turn-around public sector companies that have a potential for revival.

The government has also decided to establish a Board for Reconstruction of Public Sector Enterprises (BRPSE) to advise the government on the ways and means for strengthening public sector enterprises (PSE's) and making them autonomous and more professional. The Board would also advise the government on disinvestment, closure or sale of chronically sick and loss making public sector companies that have no chance for revival. The Board would also suggest ways and means of funding schemes for financial and organisational restructuring of certain public sector enterprises with a view to making them strong, viable and financially sound business units.

CONCLUSION

Strong views are expressed against disinvestment by some economists. However, vehement opposition to privatisation and disinvestment has continued to come largely from political parties and leaders having leftist leanings. The issue of disinvestment and privatisation is presented as an anti-people, anti-poor and anti-labour policy measure that is against the common good and larger social welfare. But the question of inefficiency associated with the public sector also cannot be just brushed aside. Even the best possible management policies have failed to make most of the public enterprises efficient or economically viable.

4

GDP as an Indicator of Development

Meaning of GDP

Gross Domestic Product (GDP) is the market value of final goods and services produced within the domestic territory of a country in a year. According to Dernburg, "Gross Domestic Product at market price is defined as the market value of the output of final goods and services produced in the domestic territory of a country during an accounting year."The computation of GDP mathematically would be as follows:

$$GDP = P * Q$$

Where, GDP = Gross Domestic Product,

P = Market Price,

Q = Final Goods and Services produced.

Features of GDP

— In the definition, the word Gross along with Domestic Product implies that the value of output is computed inclusive of depreciation allowance or consumption of fixed capital.

— It includes the value of goods and services produced by residents as well as non-residents within the frontiers of a country in an accounting year.

— The price of goods and services refers to the prevailing market price or current price at the time of production.

— Only final goods and services are included in gross domestic product. The value of second hand goods is not included. Also, it does not include the value of financial instruments like bonds, shares, etc. However, the commission earned on these instruments is included.

— GDP includes only those goods that are available in the market for sale. There is one exception: Goods for self-consumption are included in GDP whereas services for self-consumption are excluded.

— At times imputed value of goods and services that are not in the market for sale is also included. Such goods and services include (1) Rent on self-occupied houses. (2) Free residential accommodation, food, clothing other non-monetary benefits provided by employer to employees.

— GDP does not include : (1) Illegal income (2) Capital gains (3) Transfer payments (4) Windfall gains.

— Net Domestic Product (NDP) can be computed by deducting depreciation from GDP at market prices.

NDP MP = GDP MP - Depreciation

GDP as an Indicator of Development

In economic terms, GDP is a measure of the amount of economic production of a particular territory in financial capital terms during a specific time period. It is one of the measures of national income (NY) and output. It is often seen as an indicator of standard of living in a country. Changes in real GDP are generally accompanied by similar rates of change in consumption and income.

GDP is computed under two methods:

1. *Value Added Method:* In this method,

GDP = Gross Value of output (Primary Sector + Secondary Sector + Tertiary Sector) – Intermediate Consumption.

2. *Expenditure Method:* In this method,

$$GDP = C + I + G + (X-M)$$

Where,

C = Personal consumption of goods and services

I = Private investment

G = Government final consumption expenditure
X-M = Exports – Imports.

However, it has been realised after a lot of comparisons that GDP is an imperfect measure of changes in the economic well-being due to the fact that it is a gross, not a net measure (i.e., depreciation is not deducted). Practically seen, GDP does not reflect income flows between a country and the rest of the world. Thus, real net national disposable income (RNNDI), Net national product, per capita income are better measures of economic welfare.

Weakness of Gross Domestic Product

Although GDP is widely used by economists, still its value as an indicator has been controversial due to the following weaknesses:

i. Very often different calculations of GDP are confused among each other. Especially for cross-border comparisons one should be careful in using purchasing power parity method or current exchange rate method.

ii. Gross domestic product doesn't take into account the black money (i.e., monetary income which is not registered) and non-monetary benefits (where no money comes into play at all). This results in an inaccurate or for that matter abnormally low GDP figures. To quote an example of non-monetary transactions, any trade through barter system or extended services without prominent use of money.

iii. In poor countries, it may be the case that everything is cheap, except for a few Western goodies. So one may have little money, but if everything is cheap that evens out nicely. Thus, the standard of living may be quite reasonable.

iv. The quality of life is determined by many other things than physical goods (economic or not). The best things in life are free, if they are at all.

v. If many products are of low quality in terms of durability, then people will have to unnecessarily buy them again and again, thus boosting the GDP without increasing their satisfaction. On the other hand, if products are very durable then that would hamper innovation because people would be less inclined to buy new products, giving producers less of an incentive to develop themselves. Similarly, if many products are of low quality in terms of usability, and people are not aware beforehand regarding the best choice, then they will either have to purchase an inferior product or buy again and again until they find something more satisfying. Furthermore, if products have a short lifespan in the market (due to innovation or change in fashion), then this process starts all over again when people need replacement. Note that in a capitalist economy, these factors impacting the consolidation can easily cause a very high GDP figure combined with a lower satisfaction.

vi. GDP doesn't measure the sustainability of growth. A country can achieve a high GDP, temporarily, by over-exploiting the natural resources. Oil-rich states can sustain high GDP without industrialisation, but this high level will not be sustainable beyond the point where oil runs out.

vii. Incomplete accounting of consequences of action. GDP takes into account those activities also which does not add to the final output of goods and services. For example, if a factory pollutes a river, that boosts GDP, and when the taxpayers pay to have it cleaned up, that again boosts the GDP.

viii. Negative Externalities are subtracted from GDP figures.

ix. As a measure of actual sales price, GDP does not capture the economic surplus between price paid and subjective value received.

x. The annual growth of GDP is corrected by using the 'GDP Deflator', which tends to underestimate the objective differences in the quality of manufactured output over time. Therefore, the GDP figure may underestimate the degree to which improving technology and quality level are increasing the real standard of living.

Hence, GDP is problematic as a development indicator on both theoretical and empirical levels. Ultimately, using it as a proxy for development fails as it is a potential means to development and is not an end in itself. That is why it makes more sense to examine development by composite measures of the end themselves: life expectancy, infant mortality rates, literacy, education, happiness rates, etc.

5

Infrastructure Development

Meaning and Concept

Infrastructure is a set of interconnected structural elements that provide the framework for supporting the structure. The term is used differently in a variety of fields; perhaps the singlemost well-known usage is in economics, where it refers to physical infrastructure such as buildings and roads.

The prosperity of a country depends directly upon the development of agriculture and industry. Agricultural production however requires power, credit, transportation facilities, etc. Industrial production requires not only machinery and equipment but also skilled manpower, management, energy, banking and insurance facilities, marketing facilities, transport service which include railways, roads and shipping, communication facilities, etc. All these facilities and services constitute collectively the infrastructure of an economy. The development and expansion of these facilities are on essential pre-condition for increasing agricultural and industrial production in a country. Thus, infrastructure growth contributes maximum to economy growth.

Infrastructure facilities, often referred to as economic and social overheads consists of:

a) *Energy:* Coal, Electricity, Oil and Non-Conventional sources.

b) *Transport:* Railways, Roads, Shipping and Civil Aviation.

c) *Communication:* Posts and Telegraph, Telephones, Telecommunication, etc.

d) Banking, Finance and Insurance.

e) Science and Technology.

f) Social Overheads: Health and Hygiene and Education.

ENERGY

There is a direct correlation between the degree of economic growth, size of per capita income and per capita consumption of energy. Since energy is an essential input of all productive economic activity, the process of economic development inevitably demands increasing higher levels of energy consumption. The greater the degree of economic growth and higher per capita income of the country, the higher the per capita energy consumption.

There are 2 sources of energy:

1. *Commercial Energy:* These sources are commercial in the sense that they command a price and the users have to pay for them, e.g., Coal, Petroleum and Electricity. They are generally exhaustible in nature.
2. *Non Commercial Source:* They consists of firewood, vegetable wastes and dried dung. These sources are called non-commercial sources. These are renewable in nature. Both commercial and non-commercial sources are called Conventional Sources of Energy whereas solar energy, wind energy and tidal power are called Non-Conventional Sources of Energy.

The energy crises of the seventies and eighties were thus an oil crises. It was not much of a national issue but a global problem. India's energy problem is not one of demand-supply imbalance in oil only. In fact, the demand-supply imbalance is widening rapidly in all commercial fuels basically because the demand for commercial fuels has been increasing tremendously. The supply has also been increasing but not adequately. The demand-supply gap for electricity too has been widening rather than being closed. In the wake of industrialisation and agricultural growth, power demand has been growing rapidly; but on the supply side, there have been too many constraints, creating shortages and bottlenecks in generation and distribution of electric power in the country. Erratic and inadequate power supply constitutes another major dimension of energy crisis in India.

Thus, in the context of India's economic development energy crises has taken the form of oil shortage, coal shortage and power shortage. This serious concern is much widely felt in rural areas than in metro cities.

Power

Electric power, which is one form of energy, is an essential ingredients of economic development and it is required for commercial and non-commercial uses. Electric power is required for domestic lighting, cooking, use of mechanical gadgets, etc.

There are three main sources of generation of electric power: thermal power, hydel power, and nuclear power. Hydroelectric power is a renewable natural and most economised source of power. There is no problem of pollution of atmosphere or disposal of waste in the generation of hydel power. It has, however, been argued that hydel projects take a long period of gestation as compared to thermal projects.

Thermal power, which is generated by coal and oil, has always been the major source of electric power in India. Nuclear power is of recent origin and its supply accounts for only 2 to 3 per cent of the total installed capacity of electricity.

The policy of privatisation of the power sector in India till now, is regarded as a relative failure, not because the policy is really bad and unworkable but on account of opposition from trade unions and political parties and the tardy manner in which it has been implemented by the politicians in power and the top generalist bureaucrats. The coming up of BSES has improved the power supply in the capital city; still more is required in all areas at affordable rates.

Transport

If agriculture and industry are regarded as the body and the bones of the economy, transport and communications constitute its nerves that help the circulation of manpower and materials. The transport system helps to broaden the market for goods and open up remote regions and resources for production. By linking the backward regions with the relatively more advanced regions transport development helps in the better and full utilisation of resources. Expansion of transport is thus of fundamental importance for a developing country like India.

Indian planners gave high priority to the development of transport. In their opinion, "an efficient and well-developed system of transport and communication is vital to the success of a plan of economic development which lays stress on rapid industrialisation." Rail and road transport systems dominate but other forms of transport are also important within their specialised areas considering the size of the country and its geographical features. Transport development since 1950-51 has registered impressive progress but there are many bottlenecks, constraints and difficulties. Inadequacies and imbalances in transport threaten to constrain economic growth and the quality of life in urban as well as in rural India.

Indian Railways are called upon to perform the dual role of a public utility service and a commercial undertaking simultaneously. This dual role imposes on railways, on the one hand, the obligation to meet the transport requirements of all the sections of the community, and on the other hand, the necessity to generate adequate revenues to meet the total expenses of running the enterprise and also to earn surplus for discharging the dividend and other pension liabilities. Lalu Prasad Yadav has reformed railways by bringing in a lot more discipline and cleanliness.

Road transport is now undertaken by state governments, but operators and cooperative agencies. Since independence, most state governments have nationalised the bus transport system, either completely or partially. Also to provide private participation, government has introduced schemes like BUT (Built Own Transport). Railways and roads are complementary to each other much more than the other modes of transport, and are mutually helpful. Before independence, Indian shipping companies did not succeed due to severe competition from foreign shipping companies, and lack of support by the foreign rulers in

India. The performance of Indian ports does not match favourably with that of efficient ports in the Asian region.

Air transport has a significant role to play. It offers saving in time that cannot be matched by surface transport over long distances. The real progress in civil aviation started in 1920 when the government constructed a few aerodromes. There are often policy changes in the field of civil aviation and the monopoly position of Indian airlines is being challenged so as to make the air service competitive and more efficient.

Communication

The communication system comprises posts and telegraph, telecommunication system, broadcasting, television and information services. By providing necessary information about the markets and also supplying necessary motivation, the communication system helps to bring buyers and sellers together effectively, and helps to accelerate the growth of the economy.

Since 1950-51, the postal network has been expanded throughout the country, and in recent years with special emphasis on the rural, hilly and remote tribal areas. Indian telegraphs is one of the oldest government-owned public utility organisation in the world whereas telecomm is a vital input for global competition and for India's success in the international markets. It is important not only because of its role in bringing the benefits of communication to every corner of India but also in serving the new policy objections of improving the global competitiveness of Indian economy and stimulating and attracting FDI. Urban infrastructure includes water supply and sanitation that are important basic needs for the quality of life and enhancement of the productive efficiency of citizens. Few of the leading telecom companies like BSNL (Bharat Sanchar Nigam Ltd.) Bharti, Reliance Communications are major contributors of this sector's growth.

Science and Technology

Science and technology are ideas and the means with which man seeks to change his environment. While science means "accumulation of knowledge", technology represents "refinement in tools". Over the last 200 years or so, science and technology have helped to improve the quality of human life. For rapid economic progress, the application of science and technology to agriculture, industry, transport and to all other economic and non-economic activities has become essential. But there is a serious weakness in the failure to utilise the available scientific and technical manpower. The proper utilisation of the available skilled manpower has an important bearing on the promotion of research and development.

Private Investment in Infrastructure: Outlook and Prospects

Taking into account the current scenario, infrastructure investments are predominantly supported by the public sector. This is because of high up-front costs, bulky investments and long payback periods. However, the possibility of commercialisation of infrastructure investment has increased tremendously over the last decade due to integration of world capital markets and massive investment requirements. So the future suggests the introduction of a new framework of public-private partnerships in different forms.

The Government of India has increasingly realised that infrastructure need not be a public sector monopoly. The government has accorded high priority for the development of infrastructure. The role of the government has been redefined from that of an owner of assets to that of service-provider with the involvement of the private sector over the last few years.

The government has taken up a number of initiatives for the development of efficient infrastructure and towards creating an enabling environment for private participation, and enhancing competition in the infrastructure sector. All major infrastructure sectors have already been opened to private investment, and a number of private sector projects are being implemented in power generation, telecommunication services, ports, roads and airports.

Government Incentives for Infrastructure Development

1) FDI up to 100 per cent on automatic bases in most of the infrastructure sectors.
2) FDI up to 100 per cent under automatic approval route in respect of projects relating to electricity generation, transmission and dist. other than atomic reactor power plants. No limit on the project costs and quantum of FDI.
3) A Foreign Investment Implementation Authority (FIIA) has been set up for providing a single-point interface between foreign investors and government machinery including state authorities.
4) Opening of domestic long-distance telephone service without any restriction on the number of operations.
5) Hundred per cent deduction of profits and gains to undertaking providing telecommunication services on or before 31 March 2003 for the first five assessment years and thereafter 30 per cent deduction of such profits and gains for further five assessment years.
6) Full reparability of dividend income and capital invested in the telecom sector.
7) Reduction of customs duty for boosting information-technology, telecommunication and other knowledge-base industries.
8) Decision to upgrade to international standards the airports at Hyderabad, Ahmedabad, Goa, Kochi and Amritsar.
9) Income tax concessions w.e.f. 01.04.2002 in the form of uniform 10 years tax holiday under section 80IA of the IT Act to an undertaking commencing generation of power or laying a network of new transmission lines during the period beginning 01.04.1993 and ending on 31.03.2006.
10) Extension of tax benefits for urban infrastructure i.e. water treatment and solid waste mgt.

Conclusion

One observation from the above information is that the demand infrastructure continues to outpace supply. The shorter supply in this sector has to be met by creating new capacities in power, telecom, railroads, and ports via public and private joint ventures, FDI promotion. Then only is industrial growth as well as economic growth possible. We should realise that one of the biggest challenges facing Indian economy today is to set up infrastructure and to upgrade technology. Indian economy is moving on and on from developed to developing economy in the coming years. This dream can become a reality with the major focus on infrastructure development.

6
India's Foreign Trade

Meaning and Concept

It is a well-known fact that no country in the world is completely self-sufficient, i.e., no country produces all the goods and services that it requires. Due to differences in availability of natural resources and other inputs required for production, some countries specialise in production of some goods which they produce relatively cheaper than the other countries. The other countries may likewise produce some other goods relatively cheaper. Hence, countries specialise in production of those goods for which they are best suited. They produce more of such goods without prioritising the production of their own requirements and further exchange their surplus production with those goods from other countries that they need but cannot either produce at all, or can produce only at a relatively higher cost. This sort of international specialisation thus gives rise to exchange of goods (purchase and sale) across geographical boundaries of the countries. This is called International Trade or Foreign Trade.

The goods that enter into a country in the form of purchases from other countries are called Imports, and the goods that leave the country's frontiers as sale by this country (or purchase by other countries) are called Exports. The value of exports (i.e., money value of all goods exported) plus the value of imports (i.e., money value of all goods imported) during the given year is called Value of Trade or Trade Turnover. On the other hand, the physical quantities of goods exported plus imported in a year is called Volume of Trade.

INTERNATIONAL TRADE AND THE WORLD ECONOMY

Recent decades have seen a rapid growth of the world economy. This growth has been driven in part by the even faster rise in international trade. The growth in trade is in turn the result of both technological developments and concerted efforts to reduce trade barriers. Some developing countries have opened their economies to take full advantage of the opportunities for economic development through trade, but many have not. Remaining trade barriers in industrial countries are concentrated in the agricultural products and labour-intensive manufactures in which developing countries have a comparative advantage. Further trade liberalisation in these areas, particularly, by both industrial and developing countries, would help the poorest escape not only from extreme poverty but also in benefiting the industrial countries themselves.

Integration into the world economy has proven a powerful means for countries to promote economic growth, development, and poverty reduction. Over the past 20 years, the growth of world trade has averaged 6 per cent per year, twice as fast as world output. Since 1947, when the General Agreement on Tariffs and Trade (GATT) was created, the world trading system has benefited from eight rounds of multilateral trade liberalisation, as well as from unilateral and regional liberalisation. Indeed, the last of these eight rounds (the so-called "Uruguay Round" completed in 1994) led to the establishment of the World Trade Organisation to help administer the growing body of multilateral trade agreements.

The resulting integration of the world economy has raised the living standards around the world. Most developing countries have shared in this prosperity; in some, incomes have risen dramatically. As a group, developing countries have become much more important in world trade—they now account for one-third of world trade, up from about a quarter in the early 1970s.

Progress has been very impressive for a number of developing countries in Asia and to a lesser extent in Latin America. These countries have become successful because they chose to participate in global trade; helping them to attract the bulk of foreign direct investment in developing countries. This is true of China and India since they embraced trade liberalisation and other market-oriented reforms, and also of higher-income countries in Asia like Korea and Singapore that were themselves poor up to the 1970s.

Importance of India's Foreign Trade

Before independence, foreign trade was colonial in nature. In those days, the aim of foreign trade was to serve the British interests rather than India's interests. India had exported food-grains and raw material to England, and in return imported finished goods of British industries. India, thus, suffered double exploitation through that trade. But in the post-independence era the situation has altogether changed. Now the main aim of foreign trade is to serve the interests of India. Now we plan foreign trade in a way so that it may be helpful in India's economic development. In this modern age we cannot progress without foreign trade. The importance of foreign trade can be discussed on the following grounds:

1. No country can produce all goods of its requirements. Foreign trade provides the opportunity to exchange and consume the goods of other countries. It also increases the efficiency and productivity of the country's productive sector through division of labour and specialisation.
2. It is essential for India to import some important capital equipments and high technology for her industrialisation and development.
3. India's developing economy requires the import of scarce raw materials and intermediate goods with a view to maximum utilisation of her productive capacity.
4. There are some essential consumption goods, which are in short supply in our country. Import of such commodities becomes essential. For example, after independence India had imported foodgrains and other foodstuffs. Such imports are anti-inflationary in nature because they reduce the scarcity of consumer goods.
5. India has to expand her exports to pay back for its essential imports. Thus, foreign trade has an important place in the developing economy, which is moving in the direction of industrialisation.

Composition of India's Foreign Trade

Since independence, there has been a tremendous increase in the value and volume of India's foreign trade. With the continued increase in tempo of economic development, imports of capital goods, machinery, transport equipment, petroleum products, etc., have grown manifold. And since payment for imports has to be made in foreign currency, which can be earned through export of goods, sustained efforts have been made to expand and diversify exports. Consequently, there has been a sharp increase in the value of imports as well as exports that have tremendously increased India's trade turnover or value of foreign trade.

India's Major Imports

The process of economic development has brought about major changes in commodity composition of India's imports. After independence, for almost two decades, India imported huge quantities of foodgrains, edible oils and consumer goods. As the development process gathered momentum, there was a big increase in the import of capital goods, petroleum products and many types of raw materials. India's imports thus increased rapidly over the years. Some of India's major imports are discussed below.

Capital Goods

Capital goods, such as machinery, apparatus, appliances, transport equipment, etc., comprise a large part of India's imports. Since, the country required machinery and equipment for setting up of new industries as well as expansion of existing industries, and also for replacement of worn out machinery, such imports, naturally form a large part of total imports.

Petroleum, Oil and Lubricants

Economic development makes large demand for energy for running industries, transport system and for domestic usage. Petroleum products, such as, petrol, diesel, kerosene and gas are among the most widely used energy sources.

Metals

Metals include iron and steel as well as non-ferrous metals like aluminum, copper, etc. Large quantities of these metals are imported, as their domestic production is not sufficient to meet the country's developmental requirements.

Fertilisers

The significant development in the agricultural sector and the tremendous increase in foodgrains production since the 1970's are primarily based on the use of fertilisers in combination with the new technology. The use of fertilisers has thus increased rapidly. To meet the fertiliser demand, the country had to supplement domestic production with imports.

Pearls and Precious Stones

In recent years, India has become a large importer of gems, pearls and precious and semi-precious stones. This import is directly linked with India's large and rising exports of gems and jewellery in making of which these items are used.

Edible Oils

At one time, during the early years of economic development, India used to import huge quantities of foodgrains. But after the 'Green Revolution' the country has now become self-sufficient in foodgrains and hence does not import wheat or rice, except sometimes when these are needed to build up stocks. However, the green revolution has not touched oilseeds from which edible oils are produced. So, India has to import substantial quantity of edible oils.

Apart from the above, India import goods like paper and paper board, plastic materials, chemicals, rubber, medicines and pharmaceuticals, etc.

India's Major Exports

With the economic development of the country, the composition of its exports has also undergone a change. At the time of independence, the largest export items of India were tea, jute goods, cotton textiles, tobacco, spices, etc., which are called 'traditional items of exports'. Over the years, with development of the economy, the relative contribution of these traditional items of export has declined sharply. Their place has been taken by the new goods or 'non-traditional items' whose contribution to total value of exports has risen significantly. These non-traditional items include gems and jewellery, other handicrafts, readymade garments, engineering goods, etc. Some major exports of India are discussed below.

Gems and Jewellery

Gems, diamond and gold jewellery of India have caught the fancy of people in the advanced countries. This is now the largest item on India's export list and contributes about one-fifth to our total export earnings.

Readymade Garments

The export of readymade garments as a major foreign exchange earner is also a significant development in India's foreign trade.

Machinery and Transport Equipment

Rapid industrial development of India enabled the country to export light machinery, machine tools, transport equipment and in some cases, heavy electrical machinery and capital goods to mostly the developing countries.

Fish and Fish Preparations

Fish, fish preparations and marine products are another new area, which has helped India to boost her exports.

Rice

India produces some of the finest varieties of rice of which Basmati has caught the fancy of people of the world, more particularly of the Gulf countries.

Iron Ore

India has massive deposits of iron ore, which has now emerged as an item of non-traditional export.

Cotton Fabrics and Yarn

Cotton cloth and cotton yarn were among the largest export items before and immediately after independence. However, this traditional export of India has retained its significance in the country's foreign trade.

Tea, coffee, tobacco, spices, cashew kernel, oil cakes, leather, etc., are among the other items, which retain their significance on India's export list.

Direction of India's Foreign Trade

Since the partition of India, important changes have taken place in the composition and direction of our foreign trade. Many commodities that were earlier imported in large quantities have now declined in significance while new items of imports have taken their place. Similarly, many traditional exports have shown a relative decline while new exports have assumed significant position. There has also been a change in the relative share of our exports and imports to various countries signifying the emerging new economic relationships.

Direction of Imports

Source-wise pattern of imports, over the years, has remained largely unchanged. OECD group of countries, which include European Union countries such as UK, France, Germany, USA, Canada, Japan, Australia, etc., account for about 40 per cent of our imports. USA continues to be the single largest source of India's imports amongst all the countries, both within and outside the OECD. United Kingdom, which was the largest source of imports into India in the pre-independence days, has gone down in significance. As a group, OPEC nations account for a significant of India's imports due to heavy imports of petroleum, oils and lubricants. However, its share too has declined substantially since 2000-01. India also imports heavily from other less developed countries.

i) *Petroleum, Oils and Lubricants (POL).* In the commodity composition of India's imports, petroleum oil and lubricants form the largest item with a share varying between one-fourth to one-fifth in India's total import bill.

ii) *Capital Goods.* Capital goods group, including machinery, manufacture of metals and transport equipment is the other large item on India's import list accounting for about 22 per cent of imports in 1990-91. However, the share of these goods has declined.

iii) *Food and Allied Products.* The group comprising food and allied products, viz., cereals, pulses, edible oils, etc., which was on a high side during the early years, has been reduced to comparative insignificance due to successively good harvests and the comfortable production and stock position. Even though India does not import cereals now, pulses and edible oils continue to be imported.

iv) *Fertilisers.* Fertilisers occupied an important place in India's import trade due to growing needs of agriculture consequent to the green revolution. However domestic production of fertilisers has increased substantially over time. This is reflected in its declining share in the import bill.

v) *Iron and Steel.* In the case of iron and steel, where the indigenous production is coming up to keep pace with growing demand, the share of imports of this group has shown some decline.

Direction of Exports

Significant changes have taken place in the direction of India's exports since independence. There has been a remarkable expansion in our exports to Japan, OPEC nations and the non-OPEC developing countries. Though the USA still continues to be our principal buyer, the overall trend in our exports shows that we are gravitating more towards Eastern Europe and Southeast Asia, rather than Western Europe and North America. USA, with its around 18 per cent share in India's exports continues to be our principal buyer, after having replaced Russia whose share now amount to around 1 per cent. The share of the OPEC countries after having declined drastically since 1990-91 has picked up marginally in the later years. The share of non-OPEC developing countries marked a significant increase in recent years. Japan has emerged as an important buyer of Indian goods in recent years.

i) *Decline in the Share of Food and Raw Materials and Increase in Manufactured Goods Share.* In the pre-independent period, our exports consisted mostly of raw materials while our imports mostly of manufactured goods. There has been a marked change even in this respect. Now the proportion of raw materials in our exports has decreased, while that of manufactured goods has increased.

ii) *Increase in Share of Non-Traditional Goods.* We are exporting large quantities of non-traditional items such as machinery and transport equipment, chemicals and allied products, handicraft goods, and fish and marine products. However, the export of traditional items such as cotton fabrics, tea, jute manufactures, spices and fabrics also continues.

iii) *Gems and Jewellery are Our Leading Exports.* Gems and jewellery now represent one of the largest commodity groups on India's export list.

iv) *Agriculture and Allied Products.* Agricultural and allied products also occupy a significant place and accounted for about 12 per cent in our export list.

v) *Manufactured Goods.* Now over three-fourths of India's exports consist of manufactured goods comprising engineering products, machinery, readymade garments, gems and jewellery, etc.

EXPORT-IMPORT POLICY OF INDIA (TRADE POLICY)

Introduction

During the nineteenth and early twentieth centuries, international trade acted as an active agent of growth of the contempary advanced countries. Free trade and export-led growth model was however abandoned by the policy makers in India, who, after independence, sought to bring about economic development through restrictive, inward-looking import substitution policies, having kept the country insulated from foreign competition and with not much development recorded. The trade policy was reformed to liberalise imports and open up domestic market to foreign competition so that some efficiency may be introduced in our production process.

India's trade policy is a direct offshoot of its dynamic economic philosophy and shifting strategy of economic development. To begin with, the development policy was geared to achieving self-reliance through import substitution and therefore the trade policy was rigidly restrictive. The whole emphasis of trade policy was on economising the use of scare foreign exchange resources by limiting imports by all possible means and preserving these precious resources for imports essential for development. Not much was done on the export front to enlarge stocks of foreign exchange in an effective manner.

The World Trade Organisation was established to eliminate trade barriers and promote rule based world trade. The objective of trade policy reforms was to integrate our domestic economy with the world economy, and the WTO sought to speed up more towards world economic integration, popularly known as globalisation, where all economies of the world closely interact with each other to bring in global economic prosperity.

EXIM POLICY 2002-2007

The Exim Policy announced on March 31, 2002, effective from April 1. 2002, contains a bouquet of concessions for exporters, focusing sharply on special economic zones (SEZs), industrial boosters, agri-exports, infrastructural developments and reduction in transaction costs. There are specific measures for encouraging exports of gems and jewellery, leather goods, textiles, chemicals and petrochemicals and electronics hardware. Emphasis has also been placed on diversification of markets, while popular export-promotion tools like the Duty Entitlement Pass Book (DEPB) scheme and the Export Promotion Capital Goods (EPCG) schemes have been retained and made more flexible. New incentives have been granted to the cottage sector, handicrafts, chemicals and pharmaceuticals, textiles and leather industries. The time granted for fulfilment of export obligation has been increased to 12 years in the case of EPCG imports worth more than Rs.100 crores.

The Mission

The Exim Policy 2002-2007, which coincides with the tenth five year plan period, aims at increasing India's share in the global exports from 0.67 per cent to one per cent over this period. This implies that the total exports will have to nearly double from $ 46 billion to over $ 80 billion achieving a compound annual growth rate of (CAGR) of 11.9 percent in dollar terms.

Agricultural Exports

Promotion of agricultural exports has been given considerable attention by the policy. Agri-Export Zones Scheme which embodies 'a farm to port' approach and under which 20 zones were sanctioned, under the Agri-Export Policy, prior to the announcement of the new Exim policy, are proposed to be supported with development of necessary infrastructure, flow of credit and other facilities for promoting agro exports.

SEZ

Under the Special Economic Zone Scheme announced in 2000, four existing EPZs were converted into SEZ and 13 new SEZs were given approval (as on 31-03-2002). The current exim policy offers several fiscal incentives to units in the SEZs. Other proposals include exemption to SEZ units from external commercial borrowings restrictions, and freedom to make overseas investment and carry out commodity hedging. For the first time in India, Overseas Banking Units (OBUs) will be permitted to be set up in SEZs. These units, which would be virtually foreign branches of Indian banks but located in India, would be exempt from CRR and SLR and would give access to SEZ units and SEZ developers to international finances at international rates.

Towns of Exports Excellence

A number of industrial cluster-towns are exporting a substantial portion of their products, which are world-class. A beginning is being made to consider industrial cluster-towns such as Tirupur for hosiery, Panipat for woollen blanket, Ludhiana for woollen knitwear to be eligible for the following benefits: Common service providers in these areas shall be entitled for facility of EPCG scheme, recognised associations of units will be able to access the funds under the market access initiative scheme for creating focused technological services. Further, such areas will receive priority for assistance for identified critical infrastructure gaps from the scheme on central assistance to state.

Special Focus on Cottage Sector and Handicrafts

The following facilities will be made available to them: Initially an amount of Rs. 5 crores has been earmarked for promoting cottage sector exports coming under the KVIC. The units in the handicrafts sector can also access funds from Market Access Initiative (MAI) scheme for normally permissible activities including development of website for virtual exhibition. Under the EPCG scheme, these units will not be required to maintain average level of exports. These units shall be entitled to the benefits of export house status on achieving lower average export performance of Rs. 5 crores as against Rs. 15 crores for others.

Reduction in Transaction Cost, Time, etc

The new policy contains several initiatives to immunise the export sector against our disadvantages arising from the state of infrastructure, power tariffs, interest rates, industrial relations, taxation structure, etc. Further, some states have taken steps towards differential treatment for export-oriented units in matters pertaining to industrial relations to enable them to adhere to rigorous delivery schedules. The simplification of the exim policy schemes being announced in the new policy will more effectively rebate all indirect taxes on imports.

Exim Policy 2004-2009

A new five-year export import policy for five year period 2004-09 was announced on August 31, 2004.

With foreign trade largely freed and import duties falling progressively, the policy has necessarily restricted itself to a facilitating role. Although it reflects no major departure from the five-year Exim Policy, 2002-07, it however attempts to give trade a more holistic definition. It sees trade not as end in itself; but a means to economic growth. Exports are not just for dollar-generation, but are an engine of growth that can create incremental economic activity in the country. The policy, therefore, sets a broader objective of doubling India's share in global merchandise trade by 2008-09 to 1.5 per cent and giving a big push to employment generation.

To achieve these goals, the policy highlights the need to unshackle controls and simplify procedures. The major initiatives in the policy include the following:

Special Duty-free Schemes for Farm Sector

An express thrust of the policy is on the exports of farm produce. While exporters of specified farm goods would benefit from a new duty-free-credit entitlement up to 5 per cent of the FOB value of exports, all other agriculture product exporters would be allowed to import capital goods free of duty under the EPCG scheme.

Special Focus Initiatives for Employment Intensive Sectors

These comprise areas such as gems and jewellery, handlooms, handicrafts, leather and footwear. Exports from Small and Medium Exporters (SMEs) have been given a fillip. The threshold to become a status-holder exporter has been brought down from Rs.45 crores to Rs.15 crores and export clusters of Rs.250 crores turnover (as Rs.1,000 crores till or hitherto) have been qualified as "towns of export excellence". SMEs would also benefit from the liberalisation of imports of capital goods and the additional-flexibilities—for fulfilment of export obligation under the EPCG scheme.

New Export Promotion Schemes

Three new export promotion schemes have been introduced. These are: (i) A Target Plus, (ii) Vishesh Krishi Upaj Yojna, and (iii) Served From India.

— *Target Plus.* This scheme gives incentives based on incremental export growth. Under this scheme special incentives have been provided to all exporters who exceed the normal export target growth of 16 per cent fixed by the commerce ministry for 2004-05. For instance, if a firm shows a 25 per cent growth in exports will get duty free credit totaling 10 per cent of the value of incremental exports. The duty free credit entitlement goes up to 15 per cent of incremental exports if exports grow by 100 per cent during the year. This is expected to incentivise exporters to achieve a quantum-growth in exports.

— *Vishesh Krishi Upaj Yojna.* Duty-free credit entitlement of 5 per cent FOB value of exports—for exporters of fruits, vegetables, flowers and minor forest produce—would be available, and these would be freely transferable and can be used for import of inputs and goods.

— *Served from India.* Under this scheme, which is in fact a modified version of an existing scheme, the policy tries to create a powerful brand for Indian services exports in the global market. It would impact all tradable services covered under the General Agreement of Trade in Services, though the government's efforts would focus on non-IT services as the latter has already established itself. The government also reserves the right .to specify from time to time the category or type of service exports that are eligible as well as the goods which do not qualify.

Duty Entitlement Passbook Scheme to be Phased out

While putting the WTO incompatible DEPB Scheme on notice (a new scheme by April 1, 2005), the policy adopts the principle that duties and levies would not be exported. Marking a beginning towards this, EOUs have been exempted from service tax, while other exporters would be refunded service tax paid on inputs for export production.

Biotech Parks

On the lines of the IT industry conquest of the global markets made possible through the timely Software Technology Parks, the government has crafted a similar formula for service sector, biotechnology. All facilities available to 100 per cent EOUs will be extended to biotech companies located in these parts. Gradually the sops would be fashioned in such a manner as to bring Biotechnology on par with IT.

Capital Goods Imports Liberalised

In this area, major initiatives can be identified as follows:

— Norms under EPCG scheme have been liberalised
— Capital goods would be allowed to be imported duty free for export of agri-products and their value-added variants.
— Export obligations on EPCG licenses with duty up to Rs.100 crores or more have been reduced from 8 years to 12 years.
— Age restriction for the import of second-hand capital goods has been removed.
— Other changes include incentivising and facilitating technological upgradation.

New Scheme to Establish Free Trade and Warehousing Zones with 100 per cent FDI

The FTWZs are meant to create trade-related infrastructure. They would be developed as trading the lines of the existing zones in the Middle East and any other countries. The FTWZs will enjoy all benefits of SEZs, which are manufacturing hubs. The underlying principle is to recognise sophisticated warehousing and trading as services.

Proposals for setting up of warehousing zones could be made by public sector undertaking or by joint ventures in technical collaborations with experienced infrastructure developers. The government has permitted 100% foreign direct investment in the development and establishment of the zones and their infrastructure facilities.

Simplification of Norms

There is a focus on procedure simplification and rationalisation of measures for the exporter. This, in the long run, would reduce transaction cost for the exporters. The policy focuses on reduction in the number of forms to be submitted in case of application for import of restricted items, EPCG license, fixation of DEPB rates, grant of advance licence and export of restricted licence. All exporters with minimum turnover of Rs.5. crores and good track record shall be exempt from furnishing bank guarantee in any of the schemes, so as to reduce their transaction costs. In addition, all goods and services exported, including those from DTA units, shall be exempt from service tax.

The validity of all licences/entitlements issued under various schemes has been increased to a uniform 24 months while the number of returns and forms to be filed by the exporter has been reduced. This process shall be continued in consultation with customs and excise departments.

7

Balance of Payment Crises and the New Economic Policy

Meaning and Concept

Balance of Payments (BOP) is a systematic record of a country's all-economic transactions with the rest of the world in a given year. All payments and receipts of foreign exchange arising from such transactions are listed in the balance of payment accounts. It is, thus, a complete statement of a country's payments and receipts of foreign exchange in the given period of one year.

BOP has two main accounts, viz., current account and capital account. Current account records all transactions in goods (export and import of goods), which are also called transactions in 'visibles'. It also records transactions in 'invisibles', i.e., receipts and payments arising out of trade in services and other invisible items such as interests, dividends, tourist travel, etc. The difference in total receipts and total payments on account of visibles plus invisibles is called balance on current account of BOP, which could be a deficit when receipts fall short of payments or surplus when it is the other way round.

Capital account records all transactions relating to capital inflows. It records foreign aid received or given, all external commercial borrowings, flow of foreign direct investment, etc. Thus, it records all capital receipts and capital payments.

The total of two accounts, viz., current account and capital account is called complete BOP account. If total BOP receipts are more than payments; the excess goes to a third account, viz., Foreign Exchange Reserves. And when payments exceed receipts, there is a depletion of foreign exchange reserves.

Current Account of Balance of Payments

All receipts from the invisibles are added up and so are all payments. From total receipts, we deduct the total payments and get the balance on invisible account or the net receipts from invisibles. By adding trade balance (balance on visible account) and net invisible receipts (balance on invisible account) we get Current Account of Balance of Payments. It is called current account because it records transactions that are a normal source of receipt and payments of foreign currency and thus do not involve any borrowing, lending and other capital transactions. The current account is similar to the revenue account of the budget of Government of India, which shows normal channels of revenue and expenditure, while the capital account contains various types of borrowings, loans and investments.

Surplus or Deficit on Current Account

If total receipts on the current account of balance of payments are more than the total payments, there is said to be a surplus in current account. But if payments exceed receipts, the current account is said to be in deficit. The deficit in the current account of balance of payments means that the country has, during the year, spent more than what it earned in the form of foreign exchange. But how can a country spend more than what it has earned? It can do so only by borrowing from others, or finding some other avenues to get foreign exchange. These borrowings, loans, investments, etc., form the capital account of balance of payments.

Capital Account of Balance of Payments

Capital account is a record of capital transfers, such as loans and investments between one country and the rest of the world. The government of a country may borrow funds from foreign governments and international institutions like the World Bank. These are called official capital transfers. Similarly, private organisations and individuals may also take loans from institutions in other countries that are recorded under private capital transfers. Apart from loans, foreign companies may make direct investment in this country, which is called foreign direct investment (FDI). In all these ways, foreign exchange comes into a country. So, this is an item recorded as 'capital receipts'. Similarly, when the government or people of this country give loans to foreign governments and people or this country's entrepreneurs invest abroad, it involves transfer of foreign currency and is recorded as a 'capital payments'. Capital receipts minus capital payments give net 'capital receipts' or balance on capital account.

Under the balance of trade, only transactions in merchandise (i.e., import and export of goods) are recorded. But merchandise (goods) is only one of the many items on account of which a country has to make payment or receive it. There are many other items such as shipping and insurance services, interest and dividends, tourist traffic, etc., which give rise to payments or receipts of foreign exchange. They too are recorded, along with many others, to make a complete statement of accounts of how much foreign currency a country has to pay and how much it is to receive in a given year. Hence, balance of payments is a wider concept than balance of trade; it includes balance of trade along with many other items, which give rise to payments and receipts of foreign exchange.

Transactions or Items Recorded in the Balance of Payments Accounts

All transactions or items, which give rise to receipt of or payment in foreign currency for a country, are recorded in the balance of payments. Some of these items or transactions are discussed below:

Visibles or Trade in Goods

Visible items refer to merchandise or goods. Since, a major part of international economic transactions are in the form of import and export of goods, payments for imports and receipt from exports form a large component of total payments and receipts of a country, respectively. Import of goods gives rise to payments while export of goods brings receipts of foreign currency to a country.

Balance of Trade

The difference between receipts and payments (value of exports minus value of imports) is called balance of trade. This export and import of goods or trade balance forms a part of the balance of payments. The trade balance is also called the balance on visible account as export and import of goods is also called merchandise trade or trade visibles.

Invisibles or Trade in Services and Other Items Except Goods

Payments and receipts also arise from transactions in invisible items, i.e., items that cannot be seen crossing country's borders. Such items include the following:

i) *Services:* The three main services that are made use of in the international trade are shipping, insurance and banking services. Ships have to be hired for transporting goods from one country to another. The merchandise carried by the ships has to be insured for any loss and damage in transit. Banking services are used to facilitate receipts from and payments to foreign dealers.

ii) *Interest and Dividends:* When foreign companies make investment in India's industry and trade, the profits made by them in India have to be paid to their shareholders in the form of dividend. Similarly, interest has to be paid to foreign creditors for money borrowed in the past. Thus, dividend and interest flow out of the country and involve payment in foreign currency. In the same way, India may receive dividend and interest payments from the rest of the world for investments made and loans given by Indian companies and institutions.

iii) *Tourist and Travel Expenses:* Tourism and travel among the countries has become an important item on balance of payments. When foreign tourists come to India, they bring in foreign currency with them and convert it into our currency to spend it in our domestic market. The country thus receives foreign currency. Similarly, when Indian tourists go abroad, they have to convert Indian currency into foreign currency to spend it abroad. This involves an outflow or payment of foreign exchange. People traveling abroad for education, business or medical treatment also cause payments of foreign currency, while the foreigners coming to India are a source of receipts of foreign exchange.

iv) *Gifts and Grants.* People of a country may receive gifts from abroad in the form of foreign currency on different social, religious or personal occasions like Diwali, Christmas, birthday, marriage anniversaries. Similarly, organisations and agencies engaged in social and relief work may be getting grants from foreign donors. The essential thing about gifts and grants received is that the country gets foreign exchange. Likewise, sending gifts in cash to people in other countries and grants to institutions abroad leads to outflow of foreign currency.

Besides the above items, invisibles include remittances of money to their country by the people working abroad, expenditure on maintaining embassies and high commissions, etc.

Balance of Payment Crisis

Serious BOP difficulties arose in the beginning of 1980s due to substantial slow down in the growth rate of exports, a sudden jump in the import bill and a reduced inflow of net external assistance (foreign aid). The second oil shock which led to increase in crude oil prices from $13 per barrel in late 1978 to $35 per barrel in 1979 proved to be more severe than the earlier oil shock of 1973-74. The high crude prices caused almost a threefold increase in oil import bill between 1978-79 and 1981-82. The POL imports accounted for over half of the India's total import bill and absorbed almost 80 per cent of country s export earnings. Besides, increased import bill of POL, there was also a substantial increase in import of edible oils, fertilisers, cement, iron and steel, etc.

The export performance was, however, sluggish. The depressed export performance can be attributed to the severe international recession during 1980-83. Trade deficit increased from Rs. 612 crores in 1977-78 to Rs. 5,838 crores in 1980-81, and remained around the same level (Rs. 5,802 crores) in 1981-82. The net receipts from invisibles though, continued to provide some support, but they were grossly inadequate to fill up the wide gap between merchandise imports and exports.

The second half of the 1980s recorded still bigger trade deficits. The trade deficit in 1988-89 was Rs. 8,003 crores that reached Rs. 10,645 crores in 1990-91. Since, invisibles could not rise enough to fill up these widening trade gaps, the current account deficits in BOP continued to be large and recurring year after year, thus indicating some structural disequilibrium in our balance of payments. Debt servicing payment also emerged as a major item on the invisible payment side. From a small amount of Rs. 282 crores in 980-81, this amount rose to Rs. 3,536 crores in 1989-90, thus pushing India into a position of virtual international debt trap. The country came face to face with a real crisis situation in the wake of the Gulf War, which lasted from August 1990 to February 1991. Due to the shortfall in world oil production owning to this war, petroleum prices further shot up and India's POL import bill jumped from Rs. 6,274 crores in 1989-90 to Rs. 13,127 crores in 1991-92. The war also led to a drastic decline in private remittances from Indians working in the Gulf countries as much of the Indian labour fled from the war-torn nations. In fact, a lot of expenditure had to be made on the evacuation and rehabilitation of Indian workers.

The break-up of the USSR too had its adverse impact on India's export earnings. Thus, a combination of factors made the BOP crisis far too severe for India to handle; the country found itself in a precarious position.

The year 1991-92 again made a bad beginning from the BOP point of view. The foreign exchange reserves had reached rock bottom and the country was on the verge of defaulting on its repayment commitments. The government therefore made frantic efforts. It pledged its gold with the Bank of England and raised loans. It approached IMF for immediate relief and promised structural changes in its economic policy. In the words of Rangarajan, "For raising the needed reserves to meet current account deficit, unorthodox steps were taken, including the pledging of gold."

Balance of Payments: Crisis Management and Long-term Strategy

India's balance of payment, which had shown persistent deficits ever since the second five-year plan, assumed alarming proportions during the seventh plan period (1985-90). There was a shortfall in the invisible account as Gulf War led to decline in remittances from Indians working in Middle East countries (Iraq, Kuwait, etc.). Along with this, the rise in oil prices and the consequent heavy import bill, combined with lower exports to West Asian and East European countries, caused this severe balance of payments crisis, which not only affected the country's economy internally, but also shook international confidence in India's ability to meet its external obligations as India's credit rating had been downgraded by the international agencies. To meet such a grave situation, all out efforts were urgently required to restore world confidence in Indian economy as well as solving the BOP problem on a long-term and lasting basis.

To achieve the immediate objective of restoring the shattering international confidence, steps were taken to present an imminent collapse of the BOP situation through such short-run measures that aimed at building up sufficient foreign exchange reserves and strengthening liquidity position to meet international obligations. Thus, while trade deficit was widening and not much of foreign aid or private remittances were flowing in, the country took recourse to External Commercial Borrowing (ECB), which means borrowings at the market rate of interest from foreign banks and finance companies. Surely this type of borrowing is costlier than concessional foreign aid from international agencies like the World Bank or bilateral assistance from friendly countries. India also borrowed huge sums from the International Monetary Fund (IMF), which is said to have given funds attached with certain 'conditions' that made it obligatory for the economy to go in for some macroeconomic stabilisation measures, as well as affect some structural adjustments.

Whether these 'conditions' were attached to the IMF assistance or not, the fact is that the Government of India did chalk out and implement a comprehensive programme of economic reforms which sought to achieve fiscal correction (by reducing fiscal deficit through economy in government expenditure, reduction and ultimate abolition of various kinds of subsidies, reforming tax structure, etc.). The government also sought to bring about structural adjustments through programmes aimed at liberalisation of industry and trade, privatisation of larger segments of the economy by minimising the role of public sector and globalisation by adopting suitable economic policies that would integrate the Indian economy with the world economy. All these measures were aimed at strengthening the economy and making India a more attractive place for foreign investment, non-resident deposits and commercial flows of foreign funds.

The second objective of the strategy was to achieve a long run solution of BOP problem through increasing exports at a rate faster than the imports. Though imports needed to be restricted and reduced to the minimum level for a quicker solution of the BOP crises, yet it was realised that beyond a point, curbs on growth of imports would also hamper investment and thus harm the growth rate of production in the economy. Thus, the emphasis was not so much on limiting imports, as on expanding exports, which in turn, create a means for import as well and also serve as agents of all-round economic development. The strategy, therefore, was to maximise export earnings rather than minimising import payments. However, to achieve substantial growth in exports, the economy must take measures to get rid of its 'high cost low quality output' tag. Thus, reforms were implemented which aimed at reduction in cost and improvement in quality of production. Such reforms took the form of increasing competition through privatisation, tariff reduction, removal of controls on trade, etc., which were aimed at making goods acceptable and competitive in the world market.

Reforms were also made in the exchange rate management to ensure that rate of exchange of the rupee is determined by free market forces so that it is not overvalued, as it was during the time of exchange control system. An overvalued rupee makes Indian goods costlier in terms of foreign currency and places our exporters at a disadvantageous position in the world market. With the reforms in exchange rate management, now we have market determined exchange rate which reflects the real value of the rupee and in turn, the real strength of India in the global economy. Besides, the rupee has been made convertible on current account and steps are also being taken towards capital account convertibility. Convertibility of the rupee is aimed at integrating Indian economy with the world economy and make foreign investments easy and attractive in India.

For achieving faster growth in exports, we need to overcome infrastructural and supply bottlenecks. For exports, while we need to create a demand for our goods in the foreign markets, we also must ensure that quality goods are really made available at the appropriate place and time. For this, we need to improve infrastructure needed for production, transportation, etc. We should also pay proper attention not only to quality of goods but also to their packaging as well as the after sale services. Thus, while lot of efforts have already gone into making our exports of larger volume and value, many more efforts are required to fully exploit our export potential and sustain higher growth rate of exports.

Causes of Mounting Deficit in India's Balance of Payments

Very Large Increase in Imports

In terms of value, India's imports have increased sharply between 1950-51 and 2004-05 from a level of Rs. 608 crores to estimated Rs. 4,90,532 crores. Some of the factors that have contributed to this massive import growth are discussed below:

i) *Large Increase in Developmental Imports:* India launched its programme of planned economic development the first plan in 1951, which was only a small effort to rectify the maladies created by World War II and the partition of the country. The second plan (1956-61) was, however, aimed at laying the solid foundations of industrial development and all the subsequent plans aimed at stepping up the pace of industrialisation. The subsequent plans are carrying on this work of rapid economic development. Consequently, there has been a continuous expansion in imports of capital goods, machinery, equipment, etc. Similarly, there was an increase in raw materials, and maintenance imports such as equipment needed to replace the worn-out machinery and maintain it in working order.

ii) *Large increase in import of petroleum:* The demand for import of petroleum, oil and lubricants (POL) has seen a massive increase. Petroleum is a major source of energy used in industry and in surface as well as air transport. It is also used for domestic fuel in the form of kerosene and cooking gas.

iii) *Fertilisers Imports:* Apart from industrial development, necessary and adequate attention has to be paid to development of agriculture, more particularly to achieving self-sufficiency in food-grains. While nitrogenous and phosphatic fertilisers are produced in the country, the potassic fertilisers are entirely imported.

iv) *Import of Pearls and Precious Stones:* India imports large quantities of pearls, precious and semi-precious stones. These are then worked upon, polished and given the finished form of gems and jewellery, which has now emerged as the largest item of export of India.

Besides the above items, other imports that have contributed to India's mounting import bill include edible oils, plastic materials, iron and steel, chemicals needed in industries, medicines and pharmaceuticals.

Modest Growth in Exports

To begin with, growth of exports was quite low and insignificant. The growth rate picked up in 1970s and 1980s. Export trends show that India's foreign trade passed through an early phase of export stagnation (1961-1966) followed by modest growth (1966- 1985) and culminating in relatively higher growth phase (1985 onwards). The factors that have contributed to this largely slow and erratic growth rate of exports are:

i) *Low World Demand:* The world demand for many goods has remained low due to continuing recession and economic downturn in many countries.

ii) *Low Income and Price Elasticity of Goods Exported:* Many of the goods exported by India are primary goods such as cereal preparations, fish and marine products, etc. The demand for these does not change much with change in income or prices. Thus, when we make efforts to sell more and increase supply, prices fall but demand does not increase much. Hence, we end up earning lower value even for larger quantity sold.

iii) *Import Restrictions on Goods entering Foreign Countries:* Many countries have imposed restrictions on goods imported by them and this adversely affects our exports. Such restrictions in the form of high custom duties and other barriers by USA and countries of European Union have contributed to the slow growth of exports in India.

iv) *Disintegration of Soviet Union:* The Soviet Union or the USSR was among our largest trading partners and a big market for Indian goods. Its disintegration caused a major setback to our exports.

v) *Increased Domestic Demand:* Domestic demand for many goods that have been traditionally exported has increased manifold. Explosive growth of population since 1950-51 has led to an increase in demand. The supply side has, however, not been able to match this increased demand due to slow growth in agricultural and industrial output. Not much is left for exports as producers sell much of the output at home quite profitably.

vi) *Low Quality High Cost Production:* Since independence, our domestic producers have remained protected against competition from foreign goods because our import policy virtually disallowed entry of all such goods that could compete with our home products in our domestic market. Given a protective and captive market, our entrepreneurs made no efforts at modernisation and technological upgradation, and in bringing efficiency and cost reduction.

Measures to Correct the Deficit in Balance of Payment

The Government of India has been adopting and implementing various policies for restricting imports and promoting exports to reduce the BOP deficit.

1. Restrictions on Imports

The government of India has been following the policy of close regulation of imports with the aim of limiting their volume and value. The regulation of imports is implemented in following three forms:

i) *Licensing of Imports:* The import of goods into India was subject to licensing. All those persons who wanted to import goods had to obtain import licence from the government. The Government granted licences only for the import of those goods, which are regarded as necessary or essential.

ii) *Tariff Restrictions:* For the goods that are permitted to be imported under the licence from the government, further restrictions are imposed by way of custom duties or import duties also called import tariffs. This means a tax is imposed on the goods, which arrive at the Indian ports, and thus the price of such goods becomes higher for the Indian buyers. The higher the rate of custom duty, the greater is the price that Indian buyers need to pay for imported goods. These high prices of imported goods are expected to reduce their demand in the domestic market and thus act to restrict imports.

iii) *Quantitative Restrictions:* These restrictions take the shape of fixing the maximum quantity of goods that is permitted to be imported. Thus, the government may determine the total import quota of goods, i.e., the total amount of goods that can be imported and allot this quota to various importers. Nothing beyond the quota is allowed to be imported. This naturally limits the quantity of imports. However, under an agreement with the World Trade Organisation (WTO) and India such quantitative restrictions have been removed on many goods, while for others they are to be removed in near future.

2. Export Promotion

With the continuing large deficits in India's balance of payment and limited scope for import reduction, the only long-term solution to the problem lies in promotion of exports to earn sufficient foreign exchange to pay for our growing imports. Export promotion measures that open up wider international market for our entrepreneurs can speed up industrial development in the country under the incentive of larger world demand for our goods. Thus, effective programmes and policies to promote exports help the country to achieve the twin objectives of rapid industrial development with not much pressure on balance of payments. The export promotion measures adopted by the Government of India include monetary and non-monetary incentives, fiscal reliefs, credit facilities, establishment of institutions to help exporters as well as strict quality controls and inspection of goods meant for export. Some of the major steps in this direction are discussed here:

i) *Cash assistance:* A scheme of giving cash assistance to exporters, called Cash Compensatory Scheme, is in operation. Under this scheme, cash assistance is given to exporters to compensate them for indirect taxes levied on the imported inputs used in production of goods for exports.

ii) *Income Tax Concessions:* Income from exports is given several concessions under the income tax laws. For example, profits from exports are totally exempted from income tax.

iii) *Import Concessions:* Several concessions in imports of machinery, equipment and technology are given to export production units. Export-oriented units are allowed duty free imports of machines, raw materials and technology.

iv) *Concessional Bank Credit to Exporters:* For financing production meant for exports and also for financing exports themselves, the bank gives credit to exporters at concessional terms.

v) *Import Licences to Exporters:* Since imported goods fetched very high prices in the domestic market, as their imports were highly restricted, the exporters were granted licences for imports of goods up to a certain percentage of value of the goods exported by them. This was expected to provide added incentive for exports.

vi) *Issue of Eximscrips:* The system of granting import licences to exporters was later replaced by eximscrips. The exporters were given eximscrips equivalent to 30 per cent of the value of their exports. These eximscrips could be used to import a large variety of items. The eximscrips could also be sold in the market. Since these enjoyed a premium, the exporters could make additional profits from their sale. This could act as a great incentive to exporters.

vii) *Convertibility of the Rupee:* The system of eximscrips was also replaced by partial convertibility of rupee in March 1992. Under this scheme, exporters, who earlier had to surrender their entire foreign exchange earnings to the

Reserve Bank of India (RBI) at a rate fixed by it, were now obliged to sell only 40 per cent of their exchange earnings at the official rate to the RBI. The rest they were free to sell in the market at the market determined rate, which was obviously higher than the official rate. This indeed was a great liberalisation measure and a bigger incentive. In March 1997 even this was replaced by a system of full convertibility of rupee on the trade account. This meant that exporters were free to sell all their foreign exchange earnings from the export of goods in the market, and importers were to purchase this from the market for making foreign payments for import of goods. The scheme of rupee convertibility was further extended in 1994 to cover all foreign exchange earnings on current account, i.e., earnings from both exports of goods as well as from services.

viii) *System of Advanced Licensing:* Exporters are given advance licences for duty free import of goods used in production of export items.

ix) *Relaxation of Controls on Exports:* Controls on exports have been relaxed. Exports of many items have been decontrolled while export procedures and formalities have been simplified.

x) *Export Processing Zones:* Many export-processing zones have been set up. The units operating them are allowed free trade with other countries. They also enjoy various concessions like five-year tax holiday.

xi) *Export Promotion Organisations:* The government has set up a large number of organisations, which are engaged in the task of export promotion. Some such organisations are Export Advisory Council, Export Promotion Councils, Directorate of Export Promotion, etc.

xii) *Export-Import Bank:* The Government of India setup the Export-Import Bank (EXIM bank) in January 1982 with the objective of undertaking promotional activities in the field of exports. The EXIM Bank provides financial services to exporters and importers and coordinates the work of other institutions engaged in financing export trade. It pays special attention to export of capital goods.

xiii) *Devaluation:* In July 1991, the rupee was devalued by about 20 per cent in terms of major world currencies. This was expected to cheapen our goods to foreign buyers thereby encouraging our exports.

Balance of Trade

Exports of goods by a country give rise to revenue in the form of foreign currency. Similarly, imports involve a payment of foreign currency. The difference between the amount of foreign currency received on account of export of goods and the payment made for import of goods is called Balance of Trade. The balance of trade may be expressed in terms of foreign currency such as the US dollars. Or this may be expressed in terms of domestic currency (rupees in case of India) by converting foreign currency value of trade balance into domestic currency at the prevailing foreign exchange rate during that year. Thus, balance of trade, simply defined is the difference between the value of export of goods and the value of import of goods or more generally between exports and imports or (X - M) where X denotes value of exports and M, value of imports.

One thing that must be kept in mind is that in balance of trade we take account or receipts and payments arising out of export and import of goods only; no other receipts and payments are considered. Since, goods are also called merchandise, the balance of trade or trade balance is also called balance on merchandise account. Again goods that go out (exports) or come into a country (imports) can be seen (being loaded and unloaded on ships and moving across the frontiers of a country) and are thus visible, the balance of trade is therefore, also called the balance on visible account.

Favourable and Unfavourable Balance of Trade

When value of exports is more than value of imports (i.e., $X > M$) balance of trade (BOT) is said to be favourable or positive. On the other hand, when exports are less than imports ($X < M$) or imports more than exports ($M > X$), the balance of trade (BOT) is said to be unfavourable, or negative or there is said to be a deficit in the balance of trade.

New Economic Policy 1991

The economic policy comprises all those measures and instruments through which the government seeks to influence, guide, coordinate or control various economic activities so that the economy as a whole moves in the direction predetermined by the policy makers and planners. Thus, there are policies and instruments, which are implemented to give desired direction to industry, trade, agriculture, infrastructure, etc., and are accordingly, named as industrial policy, trade policy, agricultural policy, etc. All these sectoral economic policies put together form the overall economic policy of the government.

The New Economic Policy consists of all those policy measures and steps adopted and implemented by the Government of India which are aimed at increasing efficiency of various economic sectors; introducing competitive spirit in the Indian economy; removing bureaucratic and administrative and procedural impediments to the growth of domestic industry; opening up the economy to foreign competition.

Objectives of the New Economic Policy

The New Economic Policy seeks to:

i) Take effective steps to reduce fiscal deficit to ensure an era of relative price stability.

ii) Reduce the area of operation of the public sector and thus open up more fields of activity for the private sector.

iii) Liberalise industrial policy and abolish industrial licensing for most of the private sector industries.

iv) Encourage inflow of foreign capital by granting more concessions to foreign direct investment.

v) Liberalise foreign trade by reducing tariff duties and abolishing quota restrictions in case of many imports.

The above policy measures seek to remove the inefficiencies in the economic system and bring significant reforms in the working of the economy. Hence the New Economic Policy is also called the policy of 'Economic Reforms'.

Components of New Economic Policy

The New Economic Policy or Economic Reforms, broadly includes:

i) Macroeconomic Stabilisation Measures and

ii) Structural Adjustment Policies.

Macroeconomic Stabilisation and Fiscal Correction

The New Economic Policy aims at attaining macroeconomic stabilisation through reducing gross fiscal deficit. The gross fiscal deficit is a measure of government's indebtedness, as it is defined as the excess of total expenditure of the government over its revenue receipts (i.e., tax revenue plus non-tax revenue such as surplus from public enterprises) and non-debt capital receipts (i.e. grants and proceeds from disinvestment in public sector enterprises). When revenue receipts and grants are lower than the total expenditure (i.e., revenue expenditure plus capital expenditure), the balance or the deficit is met by the government by raising market borrowings and external assistance. These borrowings and external assistance constitute the loan of the government, and this loan as a ratio of GDP is defined as gross fiscal deficit. Thus, fiscal deficit reflects the magnitude of public debt or indebtedness of the government. The continuously increasing and high fiscal deficit shows the fiscal indiscipline of the government, which imposes high annual recurring costs in the form of interest and repayment of debt instalments. And, as fiscal deficit keeps growing, the government may fall into a debt-trap where every year a new loan has to be raised to pay back the interest and instalments of previous loans. In the face of mounting government expenditure and not much additional resources being raised from borrowings (since much or the fresh loans are being used to pay back the old liabilities and therefore net additions to available funds is very small), the government resorts to increase in deficit financing. This adds to money supply, fuel inflation and leads to increased deficit in balance of payments. The country may soon land into a debt-trap (both, internal and external) and thus may soon become a weak and shattered economy. It is in this context that the need for strict and strong macroeconomic measures was felt and incorporated in the New Economic Policy or the Economic Reforms Programme.

Reforms in Tax Structure

Major reforms in tax structure were also initiated in accordance with the recommendation of Chelliah Committee on tax reforms. The reforms implemented in the new economic policy include:

i) Rationalisation of income tax and bringing down the maximum rate of income tax from 51 per cent to 30 per cent.
ii) Rationalisation of custom duties and bringing down the peak tariff duties to lower levels (around 50 per cent) prevailing in most other countries.
iii) Reduction in subsidies on various items like food subsidies, fertiliser subsidies, exports subsidies, etc. However, the government has not been able to undertake any substantial reduction in such subsidies due to powerful farmer lobby and the vote bank politics that prevents any government from taking unpopular decisions.

Besides these, tax rates on profits have also been reduced with a view to attracting more investment, particularly foreign direct investment into the economy. State governments have been asked to improve financial performance of the state electricity boards and drastically reduce their losses.

Structural Adjustment Policies

Structural adjustment is defined as a process of market-oriented reforms in policies and institutions, with the goals of restoring a sustainable balance of payments, reducing inflation, and creating conditions for a sustainable growth in per capita income. Structural adjustment programmes generally start with a conventional stabilisation programme, intended to restore the viability of the current account and the budget, but they are distinguished from pure stabilisation programmes by the inclusion of a set of micro-economic institutional policy reforms.

The main features of structural reforms in the New Economic Policy can be described as (A) Liberalisation, (B) Privatisation, (C) Globalisation and (D) Financial Sector Reforms. These features are discussed below.

LIBERALISATION

The economic reforms ushered under the new economic policy aim at liberating the industry and trade from all unnecessary restrictions and removing all impediments in their growth arising from licences, permits, quotas, bureaucratic delays, etc. For this, suitable amendments have been made in the industrial policy, which are as follows.

1. Deregulation of Industries

Over the four decades of planned economic development since 1951, industry and trade were subjected to numerous restrictions in the form of licences, permits, controls, etc. The new economic policy seeks to abolish all such restrictions and free the economy from the shackles of the licence-permit-quota Raj. The liberalisation measures adopted in the new Industrial Policy of July 1991 include abolition of licensing requirement for industries. All industries except for a list of 18 industries were permitted to establish, expand or renovate or set up new units without acquiring any licence for this purpose. This list has been further reduced to cover only six industries for which licensing provisions are still in force.

Except for the six industries mentioned in the list, all other industries and projects, irrespective of how big investment is involved, have been freed from the provision of compulsory licensing. The industry has thus now been almost liberated from the restrictions placed by the system of industrial licensing.

2. Liberalised Policy Towards Foreign Capital and Technology

The inflow of foreign capital and import of technology was tightly regulated under the earlier industrial policy. But such a policy kept the inflow of foreign capital very small and industrial development suffered for the want of capital resources and technology. The July 1991 Industrial Policy made several concessions to encourage flow of foreign capital and technology into India, which are as follows:

i) *Relaxation in Upper Limit of Foreign Investment:* The maximum limit of foreign equity participation was placed at 40 per cent in the total equity capital of industrial units, which were open to foreign investments. Under the July 1991 Policy, this limit was raised. In some industries the ratio of foreign equity was raised to 74 per cent. Foreign direct investment (FDI) was further liberalised and now 100 per cent foreign equity is permitted in the case of mining, projects for electricity generation, transmission and distribution, ports, harbours, etc.

ii) *Automatic Permission for Foreign Technology Agreements:* The new industrial policy states that automatic permission will be granted to foreign technology agreements in the high priority industries. Previously any technology agreement by an Indian company with foreign parties for import of technology required advance clearance from the government. This delayed the import of technology and hampered modernisation of industries. Now the Indian companies could enter into technology agreements with foreign companies and import foreign technology for which permission would be automatically granted.

PRIVATISATION

Economic reforms are aimed at giving greater role to the private sector in the country's economic development. In the planned process of development in India, the public sector had been given a dominant role while the sphere of operation of the private sector was severely curtailed. The new economic policy sought to reverse this position through various policies that limit the area of public sector and give way to expansion of the private sector.

1. *Reduced Role for the Public Sector:* The role of the public sector, which was designed to be the driving force behind economic development, has now been reduced significantly. The Industrial Policy of 1956 reserved 17 industrial areas exclusively for the public sector. Besides these the public sector could open its units in another 12 industrial sectors mentioned in Schedule B of the 1956 Industrial Policy. However, under the Industrial Policy of July 1991, its sphere of operation was sharply reduced to only eight sectors; the rest being thrown open to the private sector. This number has been further reduced to four viz.,

defence production, atomic energy, railway transport and minerals used in atomic energy.

2. *Disinvestment in Public Enterprises:* As a measure to increase financial resources of the public enterprises as well as to encourage public participation in their management for improving efficiency of these enterprises, the government offered to sell a certain percentage of their shares to general public and private financial and investment institutions. A Disinvestment Commission was set up in 1996 to work out the modalities of disinvestments in the public enterprises.

Disinvestment in public enterprises is the only way to reduce the financial burden of public enterprises on the government. It is also expected to improve efficiency of those enterprises with the availability of professional guidance from the private sector that gets involved as a partner in their progress.

Globalisation

Globalisation means integration of the domestic economy of a country with the international economy. This means that the domestic economy does not remain insulated from events in the international arena and that there is free interaction with the rest of the world in matters of production, trade, capital movement, exchange rates, etc. The phenomenon of globalisation implies that a country buys from the rest of the world whatever is available cheaper elsewhere and sells whatever it can make cheaper within the country, and this trade is not hindered by artificial barriers, restrictions, curbs, etc. It also implies a free flow of foreign capital and freely determined foreign exchange rate. The new economic policy seeks to achieve the objective of globalisation through reforms in trade policy, abolition of import licensing, market determination of foreign exchange, partial convertibility of the rupee, etc. Some of these are discussed below.

1. *Liberalisation of Import Licensing:* In our country, imports have always remained subject to stringent quantitative restrictions like licences and quotas. The object of such restriction has been to limit the value of imports to save foreign exchange and also afford protection to domestic

industries thus encouraging them to produce import substitutes, i.e., domestic goods that would displace the imported goods. However, such restrictions made the domestic industry uncompetitive because assured domestic market did not induce the producers to improve quality and reduce costs. Thus, the Indian economy became a high-cost low-quality producer of goods that were unacceptable to foreign buyers and hence, adversely affected our exports.

One of the major reforms in the trade policy has been phasing out of these quantitative restrictions (such as import quotas) and liberalising import licensing. Under the new trade policy, most of these licensing regulations have been abolished and most imports have been put under OGL (open general licence) where largely automatic permission is granted to import goods. There is, however, a small negative list of imports for which licences are still needed, but this list is also being shortened over time. Thus, except for this small negative list, all imports are virtually unrestricted.

2. *Rationalisation of Tariff Structure:* Tariff structure refers to the structure and pattern of custom duties that are levied on various commodity groups. Over the years, India's tariff structure had become highly complex and the average tariff was much above that in most of other countries. Following the recommendations of the Tax Reforms Committee (Chelliah Committee), the Government of India initiated the process of tariff reduction in 1991. The peak tariff was reduced year after year, and the tariff structure was rationalised in an effort to bring it in line with the tariff rates prevailing in the other developing countries.

   These reforms in trade policy aim at making Indian goods competitive in the world market by removing controls and restrictions on the country's foreign trade. It is expected that competition with foreign goods will induce our producers to improve the quality and reduce the cost of domestically produced goods. Cheaper import of raw materials may also help reduce the cost of production. These high-quality low-cost goods can offer competition in the world market and improve our exports.

3. *Reforms in Foreign Exchange Management:* Earlier all exporters had to surrender foreign exchange earned from exports to the Reserve Bank of India (RBI) and get rupees in return at a fixed exchange rate. Importers could buy foreign currency from the RBI also at a fixed exchange rate. This was known as the exchange control system by which RBI rationed scarce foreign exchange among importers of various categories of goods. But under this regime the Indian rupee became grossly overvalued, i.e., the external value of the rupee was maintained at artificially high rate. This worked against growth of our exports while it encouraged imports and thus created balance of payment problems. Under the liberalised exchange management system the value of the rupee is determined by the market forces of its demand and supply. Exporters are free to sell their foreign currency in the open market while the importers could freely buy it from there. This is called free convertibility of rupee. However, this freedom to buy and sell foreign currency in the open market is allowed only in the case of that currency, which is earned from export of goods and services, and is used for payments arising out of imports of goods and services. Free buying of foreign currency is not permitted for acquiring assets and property in foreign countries. Thus, we say, the rupee is convertible on current account only and not on the capital account. Hence, India has so far adopted only partial convertibility of rupee.

Financial Sector Reforms

The Government of India also sought to bring reforms in the financial sector, particularly the banking sector to make this sector efficient and profitable. The reforms in the banking sector were based on the recommendation of the Narasimham Committee that submitted its report in December 1991. The main reforms initiated by the government are:

i) Gradual reduction in the Statutory Liquidity Ratio (SLR) from the prevailing 38.5 per cent to 25 per cent. The SLR is the ratio of liquid assets (cash plus government securities), which the banks have to keep against their total deposits.

ii) Reduction in the Cash Reserve Ratio (CRR) from 15 per cent to 10 per cent of total deposits. The CRR is the ratio of cash, which the banks have to keep with the Reserve Bank of India against their deposits under the RBI regulations.

iii) Deregulation of rate of interest. This means that the rate of interest should be determined by the free play of market forces of demand for and supply of money and not by the administrative decisions of the RBI.

The banking sector reforms also included the reconstitution of the banking structure so that there are three to four very big international level banks at the top, followed by national level banks, state level banks and rural banks. The policy also aimed at encouraging competition among banks.

Conclusion

The above economic policy reforms are thus supposed to help increase production through industrial expansion consequent to the abolition of licensing system, and other restrictions on private sector. The scope of the public sector has been reduced and its growth is discouraged. The private sector gets all encouragement to develop and enter into fields earlier prohibited for it. This policy thus ushers in an era of privatisation or rapid growth of private sector. Removal of restrictions on free flow of foreign capital, reduction in import duties, removal of trade restrictions, etc., would encourage a free flow of capital resources and goods between India and the rest of the world. Thus, Indian economy will not remain isolated from the world economic development. It will become integrated with the world economy. This is called Globalisation. The new economic policy is thus a policy of Liberalisation, Privatisation and Globalisation.

8

FDI and FII Policy in India

Meaning and Concept

Adequate availability of capital is a necessary condition for industrial development and economic progress of a country. Capital can be obtained from internal sources such as domestic savings or from external sources in the form of foreign borrowings and investments by foreign companies in this country's economy. External borrowings, which are of a concessional nature, i.e., they carry a low interest rate and have convenient repayment conditions, are known as Foreign Aid or Foreign Development Assistance. Such assistance is generally official in nature, i.e., it is given by government of one country, or some international financial institution such as the World Bank, to the government of another country. The essential thing about foreign aid is that it is concessional in nature and non-commercial in character, i.e., the objective of aid-giving nation/institution is not to earn profits out of such loans and grants

Foreign capital or foreign investment can be broadly categorised into two components, viz., Foreign Direct Investment (FDI) and Portfolio Investment. Foreign investment is different from foreign aid in the sense that it does not comprise of loans or grants; it has no repayment conditions attached to it. Rather it is there to make profits. It is guided purely by commercial considerations.

Foreign Direct Investment (FDI) is in the form of investments directly made in industry or other spheres of economic activity of a country by foreign industrial houses or multinational companies (MNC's) with the objective of earning profits. Since, the investment is made by companies in their private capacity, it is called Private Foreign Capital as against official development assistance or foreign aid that is both official as well as non-commercial. Thus, in brief, foreign capital represents foreign savings and investments in a country's economy.

Another component of foreign capital is Portfolio Investment. This investment is made by foreign financial companies called Foreign Institutional Investors (FIIs) in tradable securities. These FIIs enter India's capital markets to buy and sell securities with a view to making speculative gains. Such investments have no long-term commitments, as is the case with FDI. These investments only represent movement of financial resources and do not have much impact on productive capacity and employment.

Inflow of foreign capital in the form of foreign direct investment has been an important source of financing industrial development in less developed countries. Big private industrial houses in advanced countries have been attracted by the lure of profit making opportunities offered by the wide and growing markets in the underdeveloped countries. Therefore, in order to earn and maximise their profits, they have made huge investments in industrial sectors of these economies by setting up their branches and subsidiaries in these countries.

Advantages of FDI

Foreign capital or foreign direct investment (FDI) by the MNC's who have such large business experience, market standing and operational efficiency can be of great benefit to the under-developed countries.

1) *Foreign Capital Fills up the Saving-Investment Gap:* We know that rate of growth of an economy crucially depends upon the rate of capital formulation. Thus, for rapid industrial and economic development, the country must save a considerably large part of its income and invest it in industry or other economic activities. But income level in underdeveloped countries is extremely low and savings are, therefore, meagre. These savings are not adequate to step up the growth rate of the economy. The gap between domestic savings and the level of investment needed to

achieve the desired rate of growth can be filled by inflow of foreign capital.

2) *Foreign Capital Minimises Balance of Payments Problems:* The underdeveloped countries that have launched economic development programmes have been facing acute pressure on their balance of payments. In such countries, developmental imports such as imports of machinery, raw materials, etc., rise sharply as the development process catches momentum. But exports do not grow much because traditional exports such as those of raw materials, mineral ores are now no more sold abroad but are preserved for growing domestic industries. New or non-traditional exports take time to pick up. Thus, there is a persistent deficit in balance of payments. Foreign direct investment means that foreign companies or MNC's bring in their own machines, plants, equipment, etc., and buy other foreign goods required for their operation with their own resources thus eliminating the burden of foreign exchange payments in this account.

3) *Foreign Capital Fills Technology and Management Gap:* The underdeveloped countries are not only short of capital, they are also far behind in the crucial spheres of technology and management skills that are so essential in the process of economic development. The foreign companies or MNC's not only bring their plant and equipment that is based on modern technology but also bring along their own engineers, technicians, managers, administrators, etc., who are well versed in most modern methods of work in their respective spheres. This inflow of expertise, skill and knowledge makes the operations of industries effective and cost efficient.

4) *Foreign Direct Investment Ensures Most Efficient Use of Capital:* The MNCs ensure efficient use of scarce capital resources. These companies with their worldwide and long experience, modern work methods and sharp entrepreneurial skills, use the capital in those ventures that are most profitable and in a manner that is least risky. This ensures that capital is used in such a manner that it yields optimum results.

5) *Foreign Direct Investment is Free from Problems of Repayment:* International flows of capital take two forms, viz., (a) international loans or foreign aid, and (b) foreign direct investment or private foreign capital. With foreign aid, the advantage is that the country can use it according to its own programmes and priorities whereas FDI is used by MNC's to maximise their own profits that may not necessarily correspond with national priorities. Thus, some economists prefer foreign loans to foreign direct investment. But over time such loans create their own problems.

In brief, foreign capital supplements domestic savings and thus provides larger capital resources for development, facilitates developmental imports and thus reduces balance of payments difficulties, brings in modern technology and managerial skills, ensures better use of capital, and saves the country from problems related to repayment of foreign loans. Thus, in most of the underdeveloped countries, policies have been so framed as to provide sufficient incentives and all essential facilities to attract foreign direct investments, and thus improve inflow of foreign capital.

Disadvantages of FDI

As the experience of foreign capital in underdeveloped countries during the past years shows, the direct investments by foreign industrial giants and MNCs has not been of much help in economic growth of these countries. Rather, it has contributed to perpetuation of economic backwardness through drain of wealth in case of the Indian economy during the British rule.

1) *Foreign Capital may not Supplement but Actually Supplant Domestic Savings:* The argument that foreign capital supplements domestic savings and thus provides more capital resources for development may be correct to begin with. But as more and more FDI comes in and MNCs grow, they, through their big size of operations destroy competition, eliminate local entrepreneurs and inhabit growth of indigenous industry. Thus, growth of MNCs may be accompanied by destruction and contraction of domestic industries.

2) *In the Long Run, FDI may Cause Strain on BOP:* The argument that foreign capital prevents strain on the precarious balance of payments position of the underdeveloped countries is also not very tenable. It is true that MNCs bring in their own equipment and plants and thus no foreign exchange payment is made by the country, thereby minimising the balance of payments difficulties. But in the long run, the MNCs may cause a strain in the balance of payments through repatriation of profits, interests, royalties, management fee, etc.
3) *Local Professionals may be Denied Access to Knowledge of New Technology:* It has been argued that MNCs bring the most modern technology, management, experience and knowledge, which the local people may be able to learn by working along with the foreign experts, and use it in other areas of the economy. But in actual practice such techniques, methods and information are kept closely guarded and the local people may not have any access to them.
4) *Technology may be Inappropriate and Aggravate Unemployment Problem:* The MNCs use modern capital-intensive technology, which is inappropriate to the conditions of underdeveloped countries. This modern technology uses more capital but absorbs less labour. In countries where labour is in abundance and unemployment is widespread, such labour-saving technology is inappropriate because it does not offer many jobs and thus do not help in the removal of unemployment; it may in fact add to unemployment by extending automation to larger areas of the economy.
5) *MNC's may Perpetuate Imbalances in Industrial Structure:* Experience of the underdeveloped countries shows that foreign capital, instead of helping in the harmonious development of the economy, has been responsible for creating and accentuating economic imbalance in the countries. Thus, while extractive industries or export-oriented production may grow, the industries catering to domestic demand may remain largely neglected, by the foreign investments.

The FDI is thus a package of benefits and costs. The benefits accrue in the form of more employment and higher real wages, higher output, lower prices and wider choice for the consumers, larger revenues to the government through taxation and gains to the economy arising from modern management, improved technology, external economies, etc. However, there are some costs associated with foreign investment that arise from concessions and incentives offered to foreign investors, adverse effects on domestic savings, balance of payments problems in the long run, etc. Thus, a country seeking FDI has to weigh these costs against benefits of foreign investment. The developing countries feel that the benefits far outweigh the costs and hence are actively seeking FDI.

India's Policy Towards Foreign Direct Investment (FDI)

Over a period of about half a century of India's economic development, distinct changes have been observed in the thrust and direction of the FDI policy of the government. One can clearly see four phases in the evolution of FDI policy framework, wherein the changing approach to FDI has emerged out of changes in economic environment and nature of the industrial policy during that period of time.

First Phase-1950-1967: Phase of Cautious Welcome of FDI

India's development strategy formulated by the planners and given concrete shape under second five-year plan was based on import substitution. Since, at that time the country was short of capital, technology and entrepreneurship, required for the ambitious programmes of rapid development, the approach to FDI was favourable. The policy was to welcome foreign investment on mutually advantageous terms, preferably through collaboration and majority local ownership. The foreign investors were assured of a non-discriminatory treatment *vis-à-vis* the domestic investors; they were also permitted unrestricted remittance of profits and assured fair compensation in the event of acquisition.

Second Phase-1968-1980: Period of Restrictions and Tight Regulations of FDI

This phase was marked by increasing restrictions on FDI. During this period, India witnessed substantial expansion in scientific and technical knowledge, infrastructure development and skill formation so that constraints of capital and technology began to ease, thus necessitating lesser requirements of capital and technology imports. There was also a steady increase in resources outflow due to gradual increase in remittance abroad on account of profits, royalties, technical and consultancy fee, etc., arising on the foreign investments made earlier. Thus, relative ease in resources position within the country coupled with increasing strain on BOP due to outgo of FDI, forced the government to adopt a more restrictive attitude towards foreign capital. Consequently, the policy changes were made that imposed restrictions on FDI without technology transfers, disallowed more than 40 per cent share for FDI in equity participation and largely prohibited foreign investment in industries where local capability was available. The Foreign Exchange Regulation Act (FERA) was passed in 1973 under which FDI was restricted in certain core or high priority industries. Thus, this was a phase of restriction and tight regulation of FDI inflows.

Third Phase-1980-1990: Phase of Gradual Liberalisation

During this period, the country witnessed a sharp deterioration in the BOP position and erosion in foreign exchange reserves in the wake of second oil shock, and slow and erratic growth of exports. This situation called for increased supply of foreign exchange resources to meet the growing BOP deficits. There was thus a need for attracting more FDI. Therefore, measures were adopted to bring gradual liberalisation in FDI policy and introducing some elements of flexibility in its approach towards FDI.

Fourth Phase-1991 Onwards: Policy of Reforms and Liberalisation

Since July 1991, there has been a major shift in the thrust and direction of FDI policy, which can be described as an open-door policy on foreign investment and technology transfer. As stated in the Industrial Policy Statement of July 1991, "Foreign investment and foreign collaboration will be welcomed to obtain higher technology to increase exports and expand the production base." Transparency and openness have been the most significant features of FDI in this post-reform era.

INFLOWS OF FOREIGN INVESTMENT IN INDIA

Foreign investment comes to India in two main forms, viz., (i) Foreign Direct Investment (FDI) and (ii) Foreign Portfolio Investment (FPI). Both these types of investment result in foreign financial inflows, but their character and nature are quite different.

Foreign Direct Investment

The Foreign Direct Investment (FDI) in various fields of economic activity results in direct capital formation in the form of plant, machinery, factories and projects on which the foreigners invest their financial resources. Consequently, it enhances the recipient country's productive capacity, and adds to the volume of output and employment. It may also help in the development of associated or linked industries and act as an agent of modernisation by bringing in new knowledge and technology. This, in turn, speeds up the growth of domestic economy, encourages exports and helps integration of domestic economy with the global economy. In brief, foreign direct investment, which also represents a long-term commitment and involvement of foreign investors in domestic economy of the recipient country, is preferable due to its multidimensional contribution to the economic development of underdeveloped countries.

Revised Definition of FDI

The Reserve Bank of India has recently revised the data on FDI flows from the year 2000-01 onwards by adopting a new definition of FDI. The revised definition includes three categories of capital flows under FDI, viz., equity capital, reinvested earnings and other direct capital. Previously, the data on FDI reported in the balance of payments statistics used to include only equity capital. The new definition of FDI thus includes:

i) Equity flows (equity in branches, shares in subsidiaries and other capital contributions),

ii) Reinvested earnings (retained earnings of foreign subsidiaries and affiliates), and

iii) Inter-company debt transactions (inter-corporate debt transactions between associated corporate entities).

Portfolio Investment

Portfolio investment, on the other hand, is in the form of purchase of tradable securities by foreign institutional investors and companies. In essence, such investment represents transfer of financial resources with a view to play in the capital market and make speculative gains. These investments are short term in nature, do not add much to capital formation, and can be more volatile than direct foreign investment. The main objective of portfolio investment, which is largely made by the Foreign Institutional Investors (FII's), is to diversify their portfolios internationally with the objective of minimising risks and maximising returns.

Foreign Direct Investment in Media

— *Government allows 26 percent FDI in Print Media*: The Union Cabinet took a major policy decision to allow 26 percent foreign direct investment in the news and current affairs segment in the Indian media and 74 percent in the non-news, non-current affairs segment. Editorial control will remain in Indian hands, and three-fourths of the editorial posts will have to be filled by Indians.

— *No FDI in news agencies*: There is no change in policy regarding news agencies, which is guided by the 1956 Cabinet resolution. The 1956 resolution prohibits foreign news agencies from distributing news directly to the India press. Such distribution is allowed only through the Indian news agencies.

— *No proposal to raise FDI in DTH*: The cap of Foreign Direct Investment in Direct-to-Home (DTH) broadcasting is 20 percent at present. This cap can be raised up to maximum of 49 percent. As of now, there is no proposal to raise the cap. DTH, which was cleared by the government more than a year ago, is yet to become a reality in the country.

CONCLUSION

FDI is important not only to bridge the big gap between domestic savings and the desired level of investment – to step up the growth rate of the economy – but also to bring in modern technologies and provide better access to markets and efficient management practices. It is well reorganised that export-oriented FDI is an important means of expanding manufactured exports for developing countries, as it helps improve the quality and competitiveness of manufacturing industries.

The degree of success of a host country in attracting and upgrading export-oriented FDI depends critically on its ability to develop domestic capabilities. To benefit fully from export-orientation FDI, it suggests that the host countries need to encourage linkages between foreign affiliates and local suppliers. There is a need to develop attractive configuration of locational advantages. Commenting on UNCTAD's annual report, noted Harvard economist, Jeffery Sachs, says that "the fact that India trails China so much in attracting FDI is a matter of significant policy concern for India, because India is missing a lot of markets and a lot of capital investment that should be going there and losing it to China."

The policymakers seem to have recognised the importance as well as the potential of attracting FDI for improving infrastructure, modernising industry, raising productivity levels in manufacturing and making exports competitive in world markets. However, despite all the measures announced over the past decade, the actual FDI inflows have remained insignificant *vis-à-vis* China and other newly industrialised economies. The reasons are not far to seek. The country has been liberalising its FDI policy in small doses, in relation to its changing business environment. In a globalising world, there is intense competition among countries to maximise FDI inflows. The degree of success of the host country depends critically on its ability to create a favourable business environment for foreign investors, by providing better infrastructure and a hassle-free policy regime. In other words, what India needs is a proactive policy if it wants to attract more FDI.

Unfortunately, the infrastructure, be it power, ports, roads or civil aviation, continues to be pathetic. There is considerable improvement in the telecom services, but not in rural areas though. Economic reforms face frequent roadblocks and prolonged periods of suspension. Even where approvals are granted, the bloated bureaucracy hampers implementation. Consequently, only about 25 per cent of FDI approvals translate into investments. Tardy privatisation of the public sector undertakings, and free electricity to a large number of customers are some of the reasons for poor FDI flows in India. In a damning indictment on the prevailing business environment, Paul O' Neil, who was the US treasury secretary, said, "Honest businessman of investors are shying away from India because of widespread corruption and bribery." India should reduce trade barriers, improve governance and economic freedom to enhance foreign direct investment and productivity. Areas that have been identified as particularly in need of reform include curbing corruption, improving the effective implementation of government policies and infrastructure.

Last year, Mckinsey, in its report "achieving a quantum leap in India's foreign direct investment" (prepared for the American chamber of commerce in India), had stated that India has the potential to attract $100 billion FDI in the next five years, at the rate of $20 billion a year, enhancing thereby the country's GDP growth rate to over 8 per cent per annum. The report also states that in such a scenario, the country would also see over one million jobs being created every year. The report suggests removal of sector–specific barriers, relaxation in foreign ownership restrictions and reduction in red tapism.

Recently, the N.K.Singh–led steering committee on foreign direct investment recommended raising FDI caps in a host of sectors and an overhauling of strategy. But, if the past is any indicator, merely raising the FDI cap or expanding the list of industries under automatic approval will not open the FDI floodgates. More important is the removal of procedural hurdles, setting up a transparent mechanism and a proper legal framework.

Foreign Institutional Investors (FIIs)

Foreign Institutional Investor (FII) is an investor or investment fund that is from or registered in a country outside of the one in which it is currently investing. Institutional investors include hedge funds, insurance companies, pension funds and mutual funds. The term is used most commonly in India to refer to outside companies investing in the financial markets of India. International institutional investors must register with the Securities and Exchange Board of India to participate in the market. One of the major market regulations pertaining to FIIs involves placing limits on FII ownership in Indian companies.

Foreign Institutional Investors (FIIs) including institutions such as Pension Funds, Mutual Funds, Investment Trusts, Asset Management or their power of attorney holders (providing discretionary and non-discretionary portfolio management services) are invited to invest in all the securities traded on the primary and secondary markets, including the equity and other securities/instruments of companies which are listed/to be listed on the stock exchanges in India including the OTC Exchange of India. These would include shares, debentures, warrants, and the schemes floated by domestic mutual funds. To be eligible to do so, the FIIs would be required to obtain registration with Securities and Exchange Board of India (SEBI). FIIs are also required to file with SEBI another application addressed to RBI for seeking various permissions under FERA.

The SEBI shall, for granting registration to the FIIs, take into account the track record of the FIIs, its professional competence, financial soundness, experience and such other relevant criteria. FIIs seeking registration with SEBI should hold a registration from the Securities Commission, or the regulatory organisation for the stock market in its own country of domicile/incorporation.

SEBI's registration and RBI's general permission under FERA to a FII will be for five years, renewable for similar five-year periods later on. RBI's general permission under FERA would enable the registered FII to buy, sell and realise capital gains on investments made through initial corpus remitted to India, subscribe/renounce rights offerings of shares, invest on all recognised stock exchanges through a designated bank branch, and to appoint a domestic custodian for custody of investments held.

The General Permission from RBI shall also enable the FII to:

1. Open foreign currency denominated account(s) in a designated bank. (These can even be more than one account in the same bank branch each designated in difference foreign currencies, if it is so required by FII for its operational purposes);
2. Open a special non-resident rupee account to which could be credited all receipts from the capital inflows, sale proceeds of shares, dividends and interests;
3. Transfer sums from the foreign currency accounts to the rupee account and vice versa, at the market rates of exchange;
4. Make investments in the securities in India out of the balances in the rupee account;
5. Transfer repatriatable (after tax) proceeds from the rupee account to the foreign currency accounts);
6. Repatriate the capital, capital gains, dividends, incomes received by way of interest, etc. and any compensation received towards sale/renouncement of rights offerings of shares subject to the designated branch of a bank/the custodian being authorised to deduct withholding tax on capital gains and arranging to pay such tax and remitting the net proceeds at market rates of exchange;
7. Register FIIs holdings without any further clearance under FERA.

There is no restriction on the volume of investment minimum or maximum for the purpose of entry of FIIs, in the primary/ secondary market. Also, there is no lock in period for the purpose of such investments made by FIIs.

Portfolio investments in primary or secondary markets will be subject to a ceiling of 24% of issued share capital for the total holdings of all registered FIIs, in anyone company. The ceiling would apply to all holdings taking into account the conversions out of the fully and partly convertible debentures issued by the company. The holding of a single FII in any company would also be subject to a ceiling of 5% of total issued capital. For this purpose, the holdings of a FII ground will be counted as holdings of a single FII.

The maximum holding of 24% for all non-resident portfolio investments, including those of the registered FIIs, will also include NRI corporate and non-corporate investments, but will not include the following:

1. Foreign investments under financial collaborations (direct foreign investments), which are permitted up to 51 % in all priority areas.
2. Investments by FIIs through the following alternative routes:
   i) Offshore single/regional Funds;
   ii) Global Depository Receipts;
   iii) Euro convertibles.

Disinvestments will be allowed only through stock exchanges in India, including the OTC Exchange. In exceptional cases, SEBI may permit sales other than through stock exchanges, provided the sale price is not significantly different from the stock market quotations, where available.

All secondary market operations would be only through the recognised intermediaries on the Indian Stock Exchange, including OTC Exchange of India. A registered FII will not engage in any short selling in securities and to take delivery of purchased and give delivery of sold securities.

A registered FII can appoint as Custodian an agency approved by SEBI to act as a custodian of securities and for confirmation of transactions in securities, settlement of purchase and sale, and for information reporting. Such custodian shall establish separate accounts for detailing on a daily basis the investment capital utilisation and securities held by each FII for which it is acting as custodian. The Custodian will report to the RBI and SEBI semiannually as part of its disclosure and reporting guidelines.

The RBI shall make available to the designated bank branches a list of companies where no investment will be allowed on the basis of the upper prescribed ceiling of 24% having been reached under the portfolio investment scheme.

The RBI may at any time request by an order a registered FII to submit information regarding the records of utilisation of the inward remittances of investment capital and the statement of securities transactions. RBI and/or SEBI may also at any time conduct a direct inspection of the records and accounting books of a registered FII.

FIIs investing under this scheme will benefit from a concessional tax regime of a flat rate tax of 20% on dividend and interest income and a tax rate of 10% on long term (more than one year) capital gains.

Policy on FII Investments

Main features of the policy on investment by FII are:

1. FIIs are required to allocate their investment between equity and debt instruments in the ratio of 70:30. However, it is also possible for an FII to declare itself a 100% debt FII in which case it can make its entire investment in debt instruments.
2. FIIs can buy/sell securities on Stock Exchanges. They can also invest in listed and unlisted securities outside Stock Exchanges where RBI has approved the price.
3. No individual FII/sub-account can acquire more than 10% of the paid up capital of an Indian company.
4. All FIIs and their sub-accounts taken together cannot acquire more than 24% of the paid up capital of an Indian Company.
5. Indian Companies can raise the above mentioned 24% ceiling to the Sectoral Cap / Statutory Ceiling as applicable by passing a resolution by its Board of Directors followed by passing a Special Resolution to that effect by its General Body in terms of Press Release dated Sept.20, 2001 and FEMA Notification No.45 dated Sept. 20,2001.

No permission from RBI is needed so long as the FIIs purchase and sell on recognised stock exchange. All non-stock exchange sales/purchases require RBI permission.

Foreign Exchange Management Act (FEMA)

Foreign exchange transactions were regulated in India by the Foreign Exchange Regulations Act (FERA), 1973. This Act also sought to regulate certain aspects of the conduct of business outside the country by Indian companies and in India by foreign companies. The FERA was widely described as a draconian and obnoxious law. Following the economic liberalisation ushered in 1991, some amendments to the FERA were effected in 1993.

The main objective of FERA, framed against the background of severe foreign exchange problem and the controlled economic regime was conservation and proper utilisation of the foreign exchange resources of the country.

There was a lot demand for a substantial modification of FERA in the light of the ongoing economic liberalisation and improving foreign exchange reserves position. Accordingly, a new act, the Foreign Exchange Management Act (FEMA), 1999, replaced the FERA.

The FEMA, which came into effect from January 1, 2000, extends to the whole of India and also applies to all branches, offices, and agencies outside India, owned or controlled by a person resident in India.

Objectives

The objectives of FEMA are:

To facilitate external trade and payments.

— To promote the orderly development and maintenance of foreign exchange market.

Administration of the Act

The FEMA has assigned an important role to the Reserve Bank of India in the administration of this Act. The rules, regulations and norms pertaining to several sections of the Act are to be held down by the RBI, in consultation with the central government.

The Act requires the central government to appoint as many officers of the central government as Adjudicating Authorities for holding inquiries pertaining to contravention of the Act. There is also a provision for appointing one or more Special Directors (Appeals) to hear appeals against the order of the Adjudicating Authorities. The central government shall also establish an Appellate Tribunal For Foreign Exchange to hear appeals against the orders of the Adjudicating Authorities and the Special Director (Appeals).

— The FEMA provides for the establishment, by the Central Government, of a Director of Enforcement and with a Director and such other officers or class of officers as it thinks fit for taking up for investigation the contraventions under this Act.

Dealing in Foreign Exchange, etc.

Section 3 of FEMA imposes restrictions on dealings in foreign exchange and foreign securities and payments to and receipts from any person outside India. Accordingly, except as provided in terms of the Act, or with the general or special permission of the Reserve Bank, no person shall:

— Deal in any foreign exchange or foreign security with any person other than an authorised person;

— Make any payment to or for the credit of any person resident outside India in any manner;

— Receive otherwise through an authorised person, any payment by order or on behalf of any person resident outside India in any manner;

— Enter in to any financial transaction in India as a consideration for or in association with acquisition or creation or transfer of a right to acquire, any asset outside India by any person.

Further, as otherwise provided in this Act, no person resident in India shall acquire, hold, posses or transfer any foreign exchange, foreign security or any immovable property situated outside India.

Contraventions and Penalties

If any person contravenes any provision of this Act, or contravenes any rule, regulation, notification, direction or order issued in exercise of the powers under this Act, or contravenes any condition subject to which an authorisation is issued by the Reserve Bank, he shall, upon adjudication, be liable to a penalty up to thrice the sum involved in such contravention where such amount is quantifiable, or up to two lakh rupees where the amount is not quantifiable, and where such contravention is a continuing one, further penalty which may extend to five thousand rupees for every day after the first day during which the contravention continues.

Any Adjudicating Authority adjudging any contravention may, if he thinks fit in addition to any penalty which he may impose for such contravention direct that any currency, security or any other money or property in respect of which the contravention has taken place shall be confiscated to the central government and further direct that the foreign exchange holdings, if any, of the persons committing the contraventions or any part thereof, shall be brought back into India or shall be retained outside India in accordance with the directions made in this behalf.

If any person fails to make full payment of the penalty imposed on him within a period of ninety days from the date on which the notice for payment of such penalty is served on him, he shall be liable to civil imprisonment.

Investigation

The Directorate of Enforcement investigates to prevent leakage of foreign exchange which generally occurs through the following malpractices:

- — Remittances of Indians abroad otherwise than through normal banking channels, i.e., through compensatory payments.
- — Acquisition of foreign currency illegally by person in India.
- — Non-repatriation of the proceeds of the exported goods.
- — Unauthorised maintenance of accounts in foreign countries.
- — Under-invoicing of exports and over-invoicing of imports and any other type of invoice manipulation.
- — Siphoning off of foreign exchange against fictitious and bogus imports.
- — Illegal acquisition of foreign exchange through hawala.
- — Secreting of commission abroad.

FERA and FEMA — A Comparison

Important differences between FERA and FEMA have been summed up as follows:

1. In FEMA, only the specified acts relating to foreign exchange are regulated, while in FERA, anything and everything that has to do with foreign exchange was controlled. Also, the aim of FEMA is facilitating trade as against that of FERA, which was to prevent the misuse. In other words, the theme of FERA was: 'everything that is specified is under control, while the theme of FEMA is 'everything other than what is expressly covered is not controlled'. Thus, there is a lot of deregulation.
2. FEMA is a much smaller enactment - only 49 sections as against 81 sections of FERA.
3. In the process of simplification, many of the "laid downs" of the erstwhile FERA have been withdrawn.
4. Many provisions of FERA like the ones relating to blocked accounts, Indians taking up employment abroad, employment of foreign technicians in India, contracts in evasion of the act, vexatious search, culpable mental state etc., have no appearance in FEMA.

Foreign Exchange Reserves (Its Importance and Use)

Foreign exchange reserves (also called Forex Reserves) in a strict sense are only the foreign currency deposits held by central banks and monetary authorities. However, the term foreign exchange reserves in popular usage commonly includes foreign exchange and gold, SDRs and IMF reserve position as this total figure is more readily available. However it is accurately deemed as official reserves or international reserves. These are assets of the central banks which are held in different reserve currencies such as the dollar, euro and yen, and which are used to back its liabilities, e.g., the local currency issued, and the various bank reserves deposited with the central bank, by the government or financial institutions.

In a non-fixed exchange rate system, reserves allow the central bank to purchase the issued currency, exchanging its assets in order to reduce its liability. The purpose of reserves is to allow central banks an additional means to stabilise the issued currency from excessive volatility, and protect the monetary system from shock, such as from currency traders engaged in flipping. Large reserves are often seen as a strength, as it indicates the backing of the currency. Low or falling reserves may be indicative of an imminent bank run on the currency or default, such as in a currency crisis.

Before making any comments on the management of India's foreign exchange reserves, it is important to acknowledge two important developments: From 1991 to 2003, India has moved from being a country that faced a BOP crisis to one that has official foreign exchange reserves to the tune of nearly $90 billion. It is a matter of pride and a cause for celebration. At present, India is a net creditor nation to the IMF. It has increased its official development assistance to countries in Africa. Trivial concerns should not be allowed to override the significance of India's achievement.

The Reserve Bank of India has done an admirable job of managing the country's external liquidity and debt position and its impact on the country's foreign exchange situation. Further, there is no dearth of wisdom within the bank on the implications of rising reserves. Any kind of suggestion or advice or concern cannot ignore this aspect.

The International Monetary Fund (IMF), in its semi-annual *World Economic Outlook*, has argued that Asian countries, collectively, hold reserves well in excess of what they need to, based on their external debt, import requirements, etc., and that such 'excess' build-up occurred mainly in the course of the year 2002.

Reasons Why 'Reserves are Excessive'

1. The accumulation of reserves in excess of what is deemed prudent or desirable has occurred mainly due to the fact that the level of reserves were deemed inadequate during the Asian crisis in 1997-98. Asian countries, stung by the experience of those years and the resulting heightened awareness of their vulnerability, decided to provide themselves substantial cushion against any future eventuality.
2. China's low-wage competitiveness seriously threatens the export prospects of many Asian nations, India included. Further, China's currency is pegged to the US dollar. Given the relative unit labour costs between China and the rest

of the world, estimates of the extent of overvaluation of the Chinese range from 25 per cent to 50 per cent. Hence, many countries tend to purchase US dollars and sell domestic currency hoping to prevent or delay the erosion of their export competitiveness. This slows the pace of appreciation of their currencies against the depreciating US dollar and boosts their official reserves.

3. In the light of the tenuous geopolitical situation, particularly in the Arab world, it is difficult to predict the future course of oil prices with a modicum of certainty. After the invasion and 'liberation' of Iraq, the price of crude oil was widely expected to drop to $20 per barrel. However, it did not happen. For a long time, the price of crude oil per barrel remained at over $30 per barrel. When it began to slide towards $25, the Organisation of Petroleum Exporting Countries (OPEC) announced an unexpected production cut last month (September). This has pushed the price back above $29 per barrel.

The situation in the Persian Gulf region remains tenuous and further deterioration in the political and security climate in the region in the course of 2004 cannot be ruled out, with its consequent deleterious impact on the crude oil price. Most Asian nations — with a couple of notable exceptions — are oil importers. Hence, they need to build in some cushion for the higher unpredictability of the oil price environment.

These considerations apply mostly to India as well. Hence, larger than usual foreign exchange reserves are to be expected. However, the issue of whether reserves are excessive or adequate is mostly a matter of judgement than theory.

However, India's Foreign Exchange Reserves are Now More Sustainable

India's growth potential is far widely recognised than it used to be. Back in the 1990s, India used to rely considerably on the inflows of Indian workers' remittances from the Gulf region. Now, happily, the situation is different. Foreign institutional investors alone have pumped in $4 billion into Indian stocks this year. Further, the non-resident Indian community is more widely dispersed now — particularly after the boom in software in the 1990s — and they are beginning to plough back their savings into India.

Further, the reputation gained in the export of software in the 1990s has attracted customers for broader services — call centres, business processes outsourcing, etc.— known as Information Technology Enabled Services (ITES).

India is emerging as a centre for manufacturing as well in some specific niche areas for global companies. All of these hold up the possibility that reserves might continue to stay high and that upward pressure on the rupee in the years ahead is a strong possibility.

If the future vulnerability to foreign exchange payments is not high and if inflows could be maintained, should the RBI stop accumulating reserves right away?

Not Accumulating Reserves would Mean a Sharp Rupee Appreciation

It would simply mean that the RBI allows the rupee to appreciate as dictated by market movements. While it might satisfy the purists or theorists, practical considerations militate against that. No country in the world could handle too much currency fluctuation (in either direction) in the shortterm. Hence, the RBI is correct in managing an orderly appreciation of the Indian rupee against the US dollar.

The recent rupee appreciation against the US dollar has already invited the expected reactions from the industry fearing loss of export competitiveness. In his speech to the National Foreign Exchange Association of India, Dr Bimal Jalan correctly pointed out that the export competitiveness of an exchange rate should be seen in the value of the trade-weighted exchange rate rather than in a bilateral exchange rate against the US dollar alone. The rupee has gained far less against the US dollar compared to other currencies and it means that the rupee has gained in competitiveness against them. India's exporters should seek to expand opportunities in those markets where exchange rate movements have given them additional competitive advantage.

Is Reserve Accumulation Impeding Indian Domestic Growth?

That brings us to another dimension of reserve accumulation. That is reserve accumulation occurs primarily because the central bank somehow attaches greater importance to growth through external demand and, to that extent, domestic demand components such as investment spending suffers. There is some merit in that criticism. However, in India, this criticism does not stand empirical scrutiny. The export share of growth in India is relatively small. The country, both in terms of size and population, is a relatively closed and large economy. Hence, domestic demand is central to growth. The criticism, if any, is that the country has paid too little attention to export growth and external orientation in the past. Therefore, it cannot be really argued that India is neglecting or underplaying domestic growth or sacrificing it for the sake of the short-term expedient of export growth. The government knows what needs to be done. Investment spending is a function of the return on capital (business growth potential) and the cost of capital (interest rates). Return on capital is also influenced by the cost of doing business which, in turn, rises or falls with the level of infrastructure support (power, water, roads, and so on), the operating and regulatory environment, labour costs and policy predictability. There is awareness of the desired state and the actual state of affairs and yet the political cycle often comes in the way of the gap between the two being plugged in a timely fashion.

Using Reserves to Acquire Foreign Assets Including Technology

Then, it is up to the government to facilitate the industry 'using' the 'reserves' to import technology and capital goods and thus scale up productivity. Further, it could also liberalise the release of the foreign exchange for purchase of foreign goods and services by domestic residents. The RBI has been announcing various relaxation measures on the quantum of foreign exchange released for travel, education and overseas health examinations and other services. As for the former, the removal of the cap on the payment of royalties and technology transfer fees is welcome. The government might also consider raising the ceiling on the amount available to Indian corporations for takeover/acquisition of foreign corporations. Foreign exchange reserves should become a useful tool in advancing the cause of Indian multinationals.

Active Investment Management of Reserves is Essential in the Years Ahead

One aspect of the management of foreign exchange reserves that lies with the RBI is the management of reserves as though they are an investible pool of assets. In such a framework, the central bank has to actively manage the risk of foreign exchange rate movement eroding the value of the underlying reserves. For that, the bank needs to form a view on the outlook for various currencies in the years ahead as well as currency substitutes such as gold and other metals and act upon it. In doing so, the RBI would be emulating the practices of investment/fund managers to manage the exchange reserves pool.

Currently, governments in the three major currency blocs — the US dollar, the euro and the yen — seek weaker currencies. However, fundamentals dictate that only the US would be granted that wish in the years ahead. Therefore, for the RBI to hold the reserves predominantly in US dollars without diversification and without active management would be to run the risk of incurring avoidable losses. The International Monetary Fund Annual report of 2003 shows that the share of the US dollar in global official foreign exchange reserves had declined from 67.9 per cent in 1999 to 64.8 per cent in 2002 while the share of the euro has increased from 12.6 per cent to 14.6 per cent during the same period. Some of it could be due to the appreciation of the euro against the US dollar. However, if some portion of the increase in the share of the euro is an indication of central banks waking up to the dangers of the unsustainably strong US dollar, one hopes that the RBI is part of that awakened club.

Obviously, the RBI cannot behave like a fund manager totally and actively shuffle its portfolio of currencies and underlying bonds. That would trigger unwelcome movements in exchange rates and nullify the intention of the central bank. Hence, discretion of the highest order would be called for. At the same time, passivity in the light of possible large-scale currency re-alignment and dollar debasement would be a needless waste of precious resources.

9

Indian Financial System: An Overview

Meaning and Concept of the Indian Financial System

The financial system of any country consists of specialised and non-specialised financial institutions, of organised and unorganised financial markets, of financial instruments and services which facilitate transfer of funds. The financial system is concerned about money, credit and finance the three terms are related yet are somewhat different from each other. Money refers to the current medium of exchange or means of payment. Credit or loan is a sum of money to be returned, normally with interest. Finance is monetary resources comprising debt and ownership funds of the state, company or person.

Financial institutions are business organisations that act as mobilisers and depositories of savings, and as purveyors of credit or finance. They differ from non-financial business organisations in respect of their dealings, i.e., while the former deal in financial assets such as deposits, loans, securities, and so on, the latter deal in real assets such as machinery, stock of goods, real estate and so on. The activities of different financial institutions may be either specialised or they may overlap. Yet we need to classify financial institutions and this is done on the basis of their primary activity or the degree of their specialisation with relation to savers or borrowers with whom they customarily deal or the manner of their creation.

According to one classification, financial institutions are divided into banking and non-banking institutions. The banking institutions participate in the economy's payments mechanism, i.e., uyethey provide transaction services, and their deposit liabilities constitute a major part of the national money supply. Banks, subject to legal reserve requirements, can advance credit by creating claims against themselves, while other institutions can lend only out of resources put at their disposal by the savers. While the banking system in India comprises the commercial banks and cooperative banks, the examples of non-banking financial institutions are Life Insurance Corporation (LIC), Unit Trust of India (UTI) and Industrial Development Bank of India (IDBI).

Financial institutions are also classified as Intermediaries and Non-Intermediaries. The former acts as an intermediate between savers and investors; they lend money as well as mobilise savings; their liabilities are towards the ultimate savers, while their assets are from the investors or borrowers. Non-intermediary institutions do the loan business but their resources are not directly obtained from the savers. All banking institutions are intermediaries. Many non-banking institutions also act as intermediaries and when they do so they are known as Non-Banking Financial Intermediaries (NBFI). UTI, LIC, General Insurance Corporation are some of the NBFIs in India.

Financial markets are the centres or arrangements that provide facilities for buying and selling of financial claims and services. The corporations, financial institutions, individuals and governments trade in financial products in these markets either directly or through brokers and dealers in organised exchanges or off-exchanges. Financial markets are sometimes classified as Primary and Secondary Markets. The primary markets deal in the new financial claims or new securities and, therefore, they are also known as new issue markets. On the other hand, secondary markets deal in securities already issued or existing.

Financial markets are often also classified as Money Markets and Capital Markets, although there is no essential difference between the two as both perform the same function of transferring resources to the producers. While money markets deal in the short-term claims (with a period of maturity of one year or less), capital markets deal in the long term (maturity period above one year) claims.

As mentioned earlier, financial systems deal in financial services and claims or financial assets or securities or financial

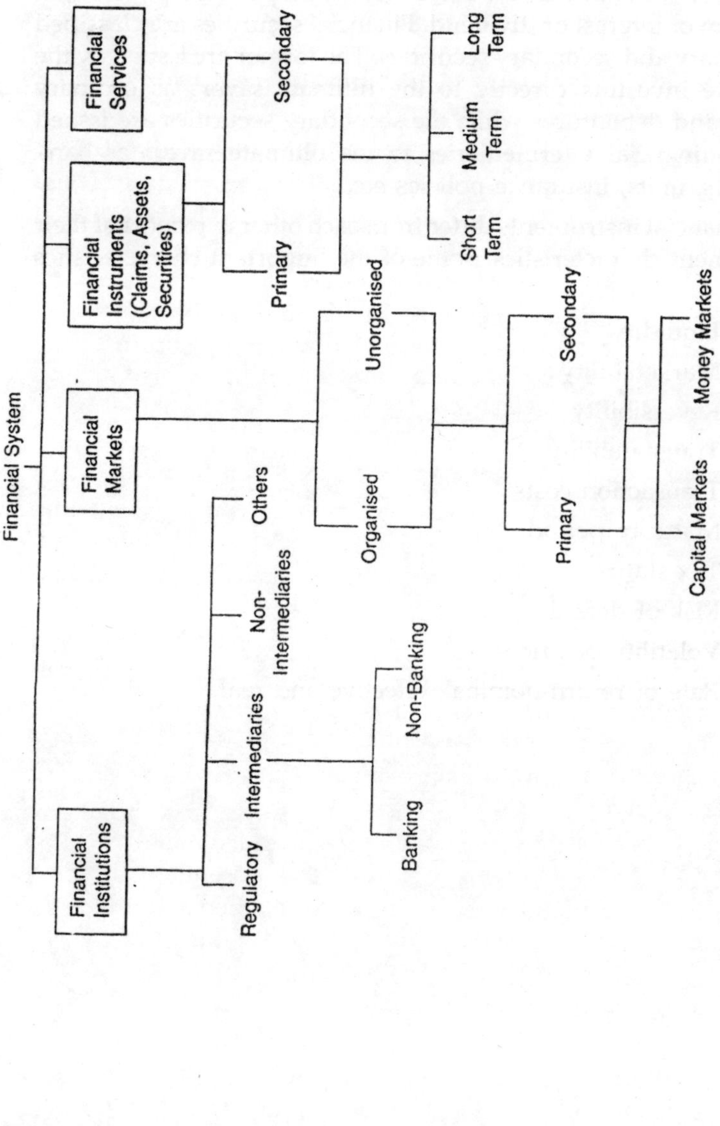

Figure: Indian Financial System

instruments. The financial services and claims are many and varied in character. This is so because of the diversity of motives behind borrowing and lending.

The financial assets represent a claim to the payment of a sum of money sometime in the future and/or a periodic payment in the form of interest or dividend. Financial securities are classified as primary and secondary securities. The former are issued by the ultimate investors directly to the ultimate savers as ordinary shares and debentures while the secondary securities are issued by the financial intermediaries to the ultimate savers as bank deposits, units, insurance policies etc.

Financial instruments differ from each other in respect of their investment characteristics. Some of the important characteristics are:

— Liquidity
— Marketability
— Reversibility
— Transferability
— Transaction costs
— Maturity period
— Tax status
— Risk of default
— Volatility of prices
— Rate of return-nominal, effective and real.

10

Indian Banking System

THE RESERVE BANK OF INDIA

Different economists have identified different functions to characterise as a central bank. An American expert, Raymond P. Kent has defined a central bank, as "an institution which is charged with the responsibility of managing the expansion and contraction of the volume of money in the interest of general public welfare." While defining a central bank, Kent emphasized only one function, i.e. the regulation of supply of money. His definition is useful as it clearly states that unlike commercial banks, profit maximisation is not its primary objective.

R.C. Hawlrey regards the function of central bank as the 'tender of the last resort' as its essential characteristics. The statutes of the bank for international settlements, defines a central bank as "the bank in any country to which has been entrusted the duty of regulating the volume of currency and credit in that country." Further, central banks of many countries have been named as reserve banks, e.g. The Reserve Bank of India, The Central Reserve Bank of Peru, The South African Reserve Bank, etc. Thus, "the custodian of bank reserves" may be considered as a function of a central bank.

The Reserve Bank of India was inaugurated in April 1935 with a share capital of Rs. 5 crores, divided into shares of Rs. 100 each fully paid up. Private shareholders in the beginning owned the entire share capital. The Government of India held shares of nominal value of Rs. 2,22,000. But in view of the public nature of bank functions, the Reserve Bank of India Act, 1934 provided for the appointment by the central government of the governor and

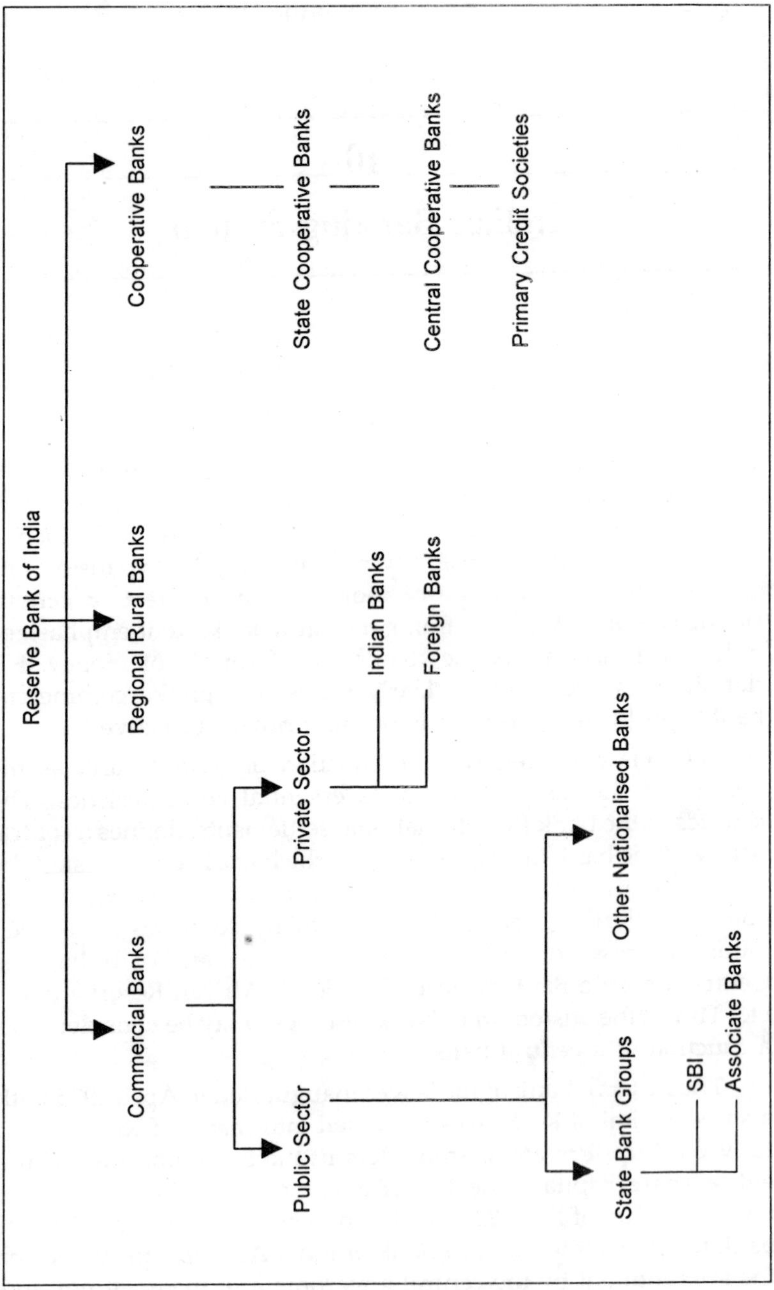

Figure 1: The Indian Banking System

two deputy governors (who are also the Directors of the Central Board). The Act also contained provisions governing the holding of shares and the rate of dividend to be paid to the shareholders. The Reserve Bank was nationalised in 1949. The general superintendence and direction of the bank is entrusted to Central Board of Directors of 20 members, consisting of the governor, four deputy governors, one government official from the ministry of finance, ten directors nominated by the government of India to give representation to important elements in the economic life of the country, and four directors nominated by central government to represent the four local boards. Besides the central board there are four local boards with headquarters at Mumbai, Kolkata, Chennai and Delhi. Local board consists of five members each appointed by the central government for a term of four years to represent territorial and economic interests and the interests of cooperative and indigenous banks.

FUNCTIONS OF RESERVE BANK OF INDIA

The Reserve Bank of India Act, 1934 has entrusted all the important functions of a central bank entrusted to the Reserve Bank of India.

Bank of Issue

Under section 22 of the Reserve Bank of India Act, the bank has the sole right to issue bank notes of all denominations. The distribution of one-rupee notes and coins and small coins all over the country is undertaken by the Reserve Bank as agent of the government. The Reserve Bank has a separate issue department, that is entrusted with the issue of the currency notes. The prerogative of note issue with the central bank of the country has the following merits:

- It brings uniformity in note issue.
- It facilitates effective state supervision.
- It avoids instability in currency.
- It facilitates control of credit.
- It ensures public faith in the currency system.
- It brings profit to the public exchequer.

— Central bank through its monopoly to issue notes, introduces elasticity in the monetary structure of the country.

Banker to Government

The second important function of the Reserve Bank of India is to act as government banker, agent and adviser. The Reserve Bank is agent of central government and of all state governments in India excepting that of Jammu and Kashmir. The reserve bank has the obligation to transact government business, viz., to keep the cash balances as deposits free of interest, to receive and to make payments on behalf of the government and to carry out their exchange remittances and other banking operations. The Reserve Bank of India helps the government both the union and the state to float new loans and to manage new debt. It acts as an adviser to the government on all monetary and banking matters.

Banker's Bank and Lender of the Last Resort

The Reserve Bank of India acts as the banker's bank. According to the provisions of the Banking Companies Act, 1949, every scheduled bank was required to maintain with reserve bank a cash balance equivalent to 5 percent of it's demand liabilities and 2 per cent of its time liabilities in India. By an amendment of 1962, the distinction between demand and time liabilities was abolished and banks have been asked to keep cash reserves equivalent to 3 per cent of their aggregate deposit liabilities. The minimum cash requirements can be changed by the Reserve Bank of India. Since commercial banks can always expect the Reserve Bank of India to come to their help in times of banking crisis, the Reserve Bank not only becomes the banker's bank but the lender of the last resort.

Controller of Credit

The Reserve Bank of India is the controller of credit, i.e., it has the power to influence the volume of credit created by the banks in India. It can do so through changing the bank rate or through open market operations according to the Banking Regulation Act, 1949, the Reserve Bank of India can ask any particular bank or the whole banking system not to lend to particular groups or persons on the basis of certain types of securities. Since 1956, selective controls of credit are increasingly being used by the reserve bank.

Custodian of Foreign Exchange Reserves

The Reserve Bank of India has the responsibility to maintain the official rate of exchange. According to the Reserve Bank of India Act, 1934, the bank was required to buy and sell at fixed rates any amount of sterling in lots of not less than Rs. 10,000. After India became a member of the International Monetary Fund in 1946, the Reserve Bank has the responsibility of maintaining fixed exchange rates with all other countries of the I.M.F. Besides maintaining the rate of exchange of the rupee, the Reserve Bank has to act as the custodian of India's reserve of international currencies. The vast sterling balances were acquired and managed by the bank. Further, the RBI has the responsibility of administering the exchange controls of the country.

Supervisory Functions

In addition to its traditional central banking functions, the reserve bank has certain non-monetary functions of the nature of supervision of banks and promotion of sound banking in India. The Reserve Bank Act, 1934, and the Banking Regulation Act, 1949 have given the R.B.I. wide powers of supervision and control over commercial and cooperative banks, relating to licensing and establishments, branch expansion, liquidity of their assets, management and methods of working, amalgamation, reconstruction, and liquidation. The RBI is authorised to carry out periodical inspections of banks and to call for returns and necessary information from them. The supervisory functions of the RBI have helped a great deal in improving the standard of banking in India to develop on sound lines and to improve the methods of their operation.

Promotional Functions

With economic growth assuming a new urgency since independence, the range of the Reserve Bank's functions has steadily widened. The bank now performs a variety of developmental and promotional functions, which, at one time, were regarded as outside the normal scope of central banking. The Reserve Bank was asked to promote banking habit, extend banking facilities to rural and semi-urban areas, and establish and promote new specialised financing agencies. Accordingly, the Reserve Bank has helped in the setting up of the IFCI and SFC; it set up the deposit insurance corporation, UTI, IDBI. These institutions were set up directly or indirectly by the reserve bank to promote saving habit and to mobilise savings, and to provide industrial finance as well as agricultural finance.

The monetary functions, also known as central banking functions of RBI, are related to control and regulation of money and credit, i.e., issue of currency, control of bank credit, control of foreign exchange operations, banker to the government and to the money market. Monetary functions are significant as they control and regulate the volume of money and credit in the country. Equally important, however, are the non-monetary functions of the RBI in the context of India's economic backwardness. The supervisory function of the RBI may be regarded as a non-monetary function. The RBI's powers of supervision have now been extended to non-banking financial intermediaries. Since independence, particularly after its nationalisation in 1949, the RBI has followed the promotional functions vigorously and has been responsible for strong financial support to industrial and agricultural development in the country.

Commercial Banks

A commercial bank is an establishment for safe custody of money, which pays out on customer's demand, order or otherwise. As per section 5(b) of the Indian Banking Companies Act, 1949 (now termed as the Banking regulation Act, since 1956), the accepting for the purpose of lending or investment of deposits of money from the public, repayable on demand or otherwise. According to this definition, banks undertake two essential functions, i.e. accepting deposits for custody and/or lending and transacting mainly banking business. Only then public will accept and acknowledge it as a bank.

Commercial banks as monopolists of the administration of payments mechanism formed by the most important segment of the Indian banking system. They are the principal suppliers of credit to the business, and the principal depository for the funds of households, corporations and other institutions. As successors to agency houses combining banking with their commercial and trading activities, they are the oldest banking institutions in India. The two basic functions of these banks consist of receiving deposits payable on demand and otherwise, and satisfying the short-term credit needs for business. However, recently they have entered the medium and long-term financing too. Among the forms of advances, cash credit is most important, followed by overdrafts, loans and bills purchased and discounted.

Functions of Commercial Bank

A modern commercial bank is a complex organisation. It performs a wide variety of functions and renders a number of services to trade, industry and commerce. It serves as a financial intermediary between the savers and the borrowers. Its importance lies in the convenience provided to them in the capacity of depository of their savings and as a lending institution.

Acceptance of Deposits

This is an important primary function of the commercial bank. The commercial banks accept deposits from individuals, business firms and other institutions, besides its shareholders. These are deposits of money and not of goods or non-money financial assets. This is economically useful function in the sense that it helps in the mobilisation of savings for production purposes. The commercial banks accept deposits in several forms according to the requirements of the different sections of the society.

Advancing of Loans

Extending loans is another important primary function of the commercial banks. It is also main source of their income. In the beginning, their lending out of deposits was confined to short-term loans to provide working funds for current business operations. Now, banks have extended their lending activities to investment in long-term bonds and open-end securities both government and private. Furthermore, today, commercial banks lend to consumers and government units besides financing trade and industry to meet the divergent needs of their customers.

Credit Creation

This is a unique function of commercial banks. No other financial intermediary has the power to create credit. By virtue of this function, banks are in a position to lend more than what is lent to them. In the absence of credit creation, the whole edifice of the money market will collapse.

Transfer of Funds

The banks provide cheque facility, with the help of which customers can withdraw any amount from their deposits to suit their convenience. Further, this facility enables them to transfer funds from one place to another. Other credit instruments like demand drafts, pay order, etc. can be used for this purpose. This function assumes significance in view of tremendous expansion of trade and commerce.

Classification of Commercial Banks

As commercial banks exist at present, they can be classified from the standpoints whether they are:

1. Scheduled or non-scheduled.
2. Licensed or unlicensed.
3. Indian or foreign.
4. Merchant banks or banks of deposits.

Scheduled Banks

According to section 42(b), a scheduled bank is one which has been included in the second schedule of the Reserve Bank of India Act, 1934. To be eligible for such inclusion, the aspirant commercial bank has to be financially and economically sound, and to satisfy for the purpose of the following conditions:

Capital and Reserves

It has paid up capital and reserves of an aggregate value of not less than Rs.5 lakhs. The expression 'value' here means the real or exchangeable value, and not the nominal value, which may be shown in the books of the bank concerned. The said bank, therefore, stands for exclusion from the second schedule, since the capital condition is no more satisfied.

Operations not Detrimental to Depositors

Its affairs are not being or are not likely to be conducted in a manner detrimental to the interests of its present or future depositors. This condition concerns itself with the functioning of the bank, its soundness and solvency. A bank is said to be working against the interest of the depositors when the management is acting dishonestly or doing anything, which is not in consonance with sound banking principles or practice.

A Company, SCB or a Notified Institution

It must be a company as defined in section 3 of the companies Act 1956, a state cooperative bank (SCB), or an institution notified by the central government in this behalf or a corporation or a company incorporated by or under any law in force in any place outside India.

Whether or not the above conditions are being fulfilled shall be ascertained after an inspection of the bank's books and accounts or otherwise by the Reserve Bank. Only when it is so satisfied that it may direct the inclusion of a particular bank in the second schedule. A bank which has been scheduled, but later fails to comply with any of the conditions described above, or goes into liquidation or otherwise ceases to carry on banking business, will be excluded from the schedule. As of today, there are 89 scheduled commercial banks, comprising 28 public sector banks, 27 foreign banks and 34 other Indian scheduled commercial banks.

Non-scheduled Banks

Obviously, non-scheduled banks are those which have not been included in the second schedule of the Reserve Bank of India Act, Generally, non-scheduled banks are small-sized institutions which restrict their activities to local areas. They are again private sector banks.

Licensed Banks

Another standpoint of dividing commercial banks in this country is whether they have been licensed to carry on the banking business or not. Till a license is not granted by the Reserve Bank, the bank can carry on the operations. But once the grant of licence is refused, it cannot be allowed to continue. The provisions for licensing are contained in section 22 of the Banking Regulation Act, and are designed to ensure the continuance and growth only of such banking companies as are run on sound lines. Those among the existing units whose functioning is unsound should be weeded out, and an indiscriminate floatation of new banking companies should be discouraged. However, the provision for licensing has been used by the Reserve Bank as a method of improving the working of individual banks rather than as a mere restrictive measure.

The conditions which a banking company has to fulfil before it becomes eligible for a licence to carry on banking business are set out in sub-section (3) of section 22 of the Act and are as follows:

Capacity to Pay Depositors

The company is or will be in a position to pay its present or future depositors in full as their claims accrue. This capacity to pay the present and the prospective depositors is the basic condition in the grant of licence. As such, the banking company is required to maintain liquid and other realisable assets on the basis of which the officers of the Reserve Bank could form an opinion about its solvency.

Operations not Detrimental to the Interests of Depositors

The affairs of the company are not being or are not likely to be conducted in a manner detrimental to the interests of it's present or future depositors.

No Discrimination Abroad

If the company is incorporated outside India, the government or law of that country should not discriminate in any way against banking companies registered in India. This could be called the reciprocity clause, which requires the foreign companies to accord the same fair treatment to Indian banks as they expect their offices to receive in India.

If the company at any time fails to comply with any of the above conditions or if the company ceases to carry on banking business in India, the Reserve Bank may cancel the license granted to a banking company.

Foreign Banks

Commercial banks are further divided into Indian and foreign, depending on whether they have been incorporated under the Companies Act in India or outside. The banks having their incorporation abroad are now referred to as foreign banks, when till the 1950's they were called foreign exchange banks since they alone transacted most of the import-export financing business. At present, in India, there are 27 foreign banks, all scheduled and very strong indeed. The foreign banks mainly provide services to the corporate sector, especially in the field of trade finance, foreign exchange, and treasury management. They also act as a point of access to their group worldwide. These include Chase Manhattan Bank, State Bank of Mauritius, Development Bank of Singapore, etc. Amongst these, British origin banks dominate the scene, with the ANZ Grindlays Bank at the top.

Merchant Banks

A bank of deposits is the one which engages itself in collecting large deposits of money from the public, and lending and investing it to the different sections of society. The business of a merchant bank (called in USA and Japan as Investment Bank), on the other hand, consists in rendering financial advisory services in consideration of fees. The range of these non-fund services is increasing fast, but broadly it includes:

1. *Issue Management:* Acting as managers to the new equity shares, bonds and debentures of joint stock companies.
2. *Project Counselling:* Giving considered advice with regard to the location, technical collaboration, diversification, tax planning, project size, market surveys, organisational and management set-up, mergers and amalgamations.
3. *Credit Syndication:* Arranging term and working capital loans from banks and other financial institutions, and making pre-sanctioned and post-sanction negotiations, providing bridge loans and loan syndication.

4. *Equipment Leasing:* A relatively new but growing business activity. Leasing finances the use of such assets as machinery for manufacturing sector, mining and construction equipment, etc. Besides, other services by merchant banks comprise management of surplus cash, project finance and capital restructuring, portfolio management, provision of venture capital, raising funds from overseas markets, factoring and over-the-counters (OTC) trading in small, odd-lot securities.

Role and Importance of Commercial Banks

Today, banks acquire a unique position in the developed as well as the underdeveloped countries. The present level of investment activity could not be achieved without the effective mobilisation of savings by the banks. There is hardly any transaction between the firms that do not involve services of banks. No economy will do well in the absence of organised monetary and credit system.

The commercial banks render a useful service to the society by mobilising the inactive savings for productive purposes. Since banks thus, have become the nerve centre of business, trade and industry, without the development of organised and sound banking system, India cannot hope to join the ranks of advanced countries. The role of the commercial banks is analysed under the following points:

Promotion of Capital Formation

The importance of banks in the capital formation process arises, as those who invest are generally different persons or institutions. Commercial banks encourage the habit of thrift and mobilise the dormant savings of the people. These savings are effectively allocated among the ultimate users of funds, i.e., investors, for productive investment. This process is termed as real capital formation. Diversion of resources from consumption to the production of capital goods accelerates the economic growth of the country through increase in the capital formation.

Provision of Finance and Credit

Commercial banks provide finance and credit for lubricating industry, commerce and trade. Establishment as well as expansion of industrial plants is not possible without enough working capital, which is provided by the banks. A number of big commercial banks financing the international trade is the result of banks' financial support, even at the international trade by advancing pre-shipment arrangements between the domestic firms to import machinery and other necessary equipment. With this, the size of the market can be expanded.

Developing Entrepreneurship

Banks promote entrepreneurship by underwriting new scrips, granting assistance as mentor for promoting new ventures or financing promotional activities under the joint guarantee scheme. The assistance of bank is also required for exploiting a new invention or for converting a private firm into a limited company or for making sick units as viable units. However, banks generally prefer to assist sound industries whose products are in great demand.

Providing Elasticity to Supply of Money

Banks through expansion or contraction of credit can effectively meet the demand for money. In the event of low demand for money, the credit can be contracted and vice versa. Banks can, thus, affect the level of economic activity. When banks issue credit money more than required, it may result in inflationary pressures.

Distribution of Funds between Regions

Commercial banks can influence the direction of economic activities through the distribution of funds among different regions. They can maximise the profits by proper allocation of funds. They transfer surplus capital from regions, where it is not needed too much, to those regions where it can be more usefully and effectively employed. Regions with growth potentials are identified for this purpose to stimulate production. However, the banks, approach towards regional growth has undergone a change. Therefore, commercial banks act as engineers of balanced regional development through disbursements of credit as per the priorities laid down under economic planning.

Cooperative Banks

The cooperative credit movement was officially launched in India in 1904 after the famous prescription of Nicholson. It represents a three tier structure—primary agricultural credit societies (PACSs) forming the ground floor, the central cooperative banks (CCBs) the middle level, and the state cooperative banks (SCBs) the top floor as the apex institutions. Whereas the primary societies deal directly with individuals, the central bank deal with primaries, are in turn dealt with by the state cooperative banks.

Cooperative banks mobilise the savings of the members and non-members by inculcating the habit and self-help, and lend the funds so raised to those who can profit by them. To cooperative banks, profit motive is subordinate to service, while the reverse is true for commercial banks. With effect from March 1, 1966, the date on which Banking Companies Act, 1949 came into force, those state cooperative banks, central cooperative banks and primary non-agricultural credit societies which have a paid-up capital and reserves of not less than Rs.1 lakh have been brought within the regulatory framework of the Reserve Bank.

However, the most disturbing aspect of the working of cooperative banks has been the poor recovery of loans. Along with the increase in the quantum of advances, there has been a corresponding rise in the overdues showing that the banking habit has not yet developed among the borrowers. On an average, over dues to outstanding advances are as high as 44 per cent. Then, a large number of PACs still remain non-viable even after their reorganisation. Their expenses exceed their incomes, and overdue loans are mounting. However, the programme of intensive development of PACs for transforming them into efficient multipurpose units, under the monitoring of NABARD, is being implemented.

Regional Rural Banks

A development of far-reaching effect on the extension of banking facilities to rural areas has been the setting up of Regional Rural

Banks (RRBs). The Regional Rural Banks ordinance 1975 was replaced by an Act of Parliament, which came into force with effect from February 9, 1976. These had in all 14,546 branches. The deposits and advances aggregated Rs.56, 295 crores and Rs.25, 038 crores in the year 2004.

These low-cost institutions aim at providing effective alternative credit facilities to the rural population, especially to that covered under the debt relief measures. The borrowers from these banks are small and marginal farmers, agricultural labourers, artisans and small entrepreneurs in rural areas. These banks form the central scheme of the economic philosophy for rural development. These have been specifically set up in districts where the cooperative structure is weak and commercial banks have not made much headway.

Each RRB has been sponsored by a public sector bank, which provides assistance in several ways, viz., subscription to its share capital, provision of managerial and financial assistance, and help in the recruitment and training of personnel. The authorised capital of each RRB is Rs. 1 crore and the issued capital is Rs. 25 lakhs. Of the issued capital, 50 per cent is being subscribed by the Government of India, 15 per cent by the concerned state government, and the balance of 35 per cent by the sponsor bank.

However, the overall performance of RRBs has been a little disappointing. Their credit-deposit ration has continuously declined and stands at present at 63.8 per cent. Their over dues have also shown a rising trend and are around 32 per cent. With a view to restructuring them, a number of policy measures have been taken by the Reserve Bank. These include:

a) Relocating the loss-recurring branches,
b) Freeing of many RRBs from the Service Area Approach, and
c) Permitting them to lend upto the extent of 60 per cent to non-target groups.

Reforms in the Banking Sector

The Narasimham Committee (1991) has offered a highly incisive and frank (open) discussion of the main reasons for the steep decline in productivity and efficiency of India's banking system, leading to a serious erosion of its profitability. About the poor state of the profitability of banks, the committee has recorded that "gross profits (surplus before provisions) have been declining for the banking system over the past decades and in 1989–90, such profits (before provisions) were no more than 1.10 per cent of the working funds." If adequate provisions were made for sticky advances and against loan losses, the situation would be a cause for serious concern.

The factors responsible for this state of affairs are discussed briefly below. They have reduced the income of banks and/or increased their expenditure; some are the product of macro – policy decisions of the authorities and others are internal to banks – their organisation, staffing and branch expansion etc.

System of Directed Investment

This comes in the form of the minimum "statutory liquidity ratio" (SLR) and the minimum "cash reserve ratio" (CRR). The SLR till March 1992 was 38.5 per cent of net demand and time liabilities (lowered to 30 per cent thereafter for any increase in such liability). In addition, the CRR is 15 per cent of these liabilities plus a 10 per cent incremental ratio (withdraw in April 1992). This had made a total of 63.5 per cent at the margin and somewhat less than this on the average. It has been argued that the SLR has diverted too much of the household savings mobilised by the banking system to finance the government expenditure – capital as well as current.

The CRR

The high CRR also depresses the income of banks, because the interest paid by the RBI on deposits above the basic minimum of 3 per cent is below the opportunity cost of funds of banks. The RBI has been paying interest on additional deposits impounded at the rate of 10.5 per cent on eligible cash balances as on March 1990 and 5 per cent on incremental cash balances thereafter, but these rates are below the current rate for one–year term deposits with banks. With well over half of bank deposits as term deposits, the loss in potential income to banks from the reserve requirement tax has adversely affected the profitability of banks.

The System of Directed Credit Programmes

It has come in for severe criticism at the hands of the Narasimham Committee. Such programmes were adopted under the development credit policy of the government enunciated at the time of the nationalisation of banks in 1969. They involved extending bank credit facilities geographically as well as functionally – geographically, over the hitherto unbanked regions such as the rural hinterland; functionally, by expanding bank credit to agriculture, small industry and the professional – the so-called priority sectors of the economy. Quantitatively the redeployment of bank credit has been, more or less the policy directions. But, as emphasised by the Narasimham Committee, this achievement has been at the cost of the quality of loan portfolio of banks, the growth of banks, the growth of overdues and consequent erosion of profitability of banks.

Concessional Lending Rates on Priority Sector Credit

This involves an element of subsidy, which is given by the excess of the normal lending rate of banks over the concessional rate. This also cuts into the profits of banks. Two points are worth bearing in mind here, one: the timely and adequate access to credit is much more important than its cost or the subsidisation thereof. After all, institutional finance, even at normal cost, is much cheaper then the informal-sector finance. Two, subsidised credit to the selected beneficiaries is at the expense of those unfortunate ones who are denied bank credit, because no bank can possibly meet the credit needs of all potential borrowers.

Political and Administrative Interference

According to the Narasimham Committee by far the most serious damage to the credit system of banks and one which has contributed greatly to the decline in the quality of the loan portfolio of banks has been the political and administrative interference in their credit-decision-making. The following grave cases of such interference are worth recording:

a) In many cases of IRDP lending, banks have virtually abdicated their responsibility in undertaking need-based credit assessment and appraisal of potential viability of aspirants for loans, and have, instead, tended to rely on lists of identified borrowers prepared by government authorities;

b) The phenomenon of loan meals was quite contrary to the principles of a professional appraisal of bank credit needs;

c) Loan waivers have added an additional element of politicisation of banking. They have also done serious damage to credit discipline among borrowers by encouraging defaults. The political element has condoned overdue of defaulters without any regard for the social obligation of banks towards their deposit-holders.

The squeeze on the profitability of banks has also come from the side of expenditure. The latter has gone up on several counts. First, the interest cost of raising funds for the banks has been going up as a result of higher interest rates on deposits and a shift in the maturity pattern of deposits towards longer-term deposits. Phenomenal expansion of branch banking which has raised several problems. The bulk of the new branches have gone to rural and semi-urban areas, where loans are given largely for agriculture and small industries and at subsidised rates. But, the unit costs of administering such loans tend to be relatively higher as compared to the costs of servicing loans to large industrial borrowers. As pointed out by the narasimham committee, extensive geographical spread of banks has tended to weaken the central office supervision of far-flung banks and any system of internal control, balancing of books, reconciliation of inter-branch and inter-bank entries and timely audit of all bank accounts.

Manpower Problems

Another problem area for banks is their manpower. With the rapid growth of banks, their offices in the number of staff was accompanied by over-manning at various levels. Acceleration promotions have diluted the quality of supervisory and managerial staff. Trade unions, besides looking after the legitimate grievances and service conditions of their members, have also contributed to the proliferation of restrictive practices. The technology of bank operations has, over the past few decades, shown little improvement, despite manifold expansion of business. This has aggravated the position of some of the weaker banks. Therefore, there is a strong case for curtailing yearly expansion of bank staff and for their suitable redeployment as among several centers.

Other Shortcomings

Declining profitability of banks has adversely affected their capitalisation, as they have not been able to add sufficiently to their own resources in the form of reserves. The ratio of capital funds of Indian banks to their risk-weighted assets is low on the average by international standard. Moreover, we are saying this on the basis of published balance sheets, when the truth is that these documents conceal much. The concealment is attempted generally by making inadequate provision for loan – losses and bad and doubtful debts in their accounts.

Recommendations of the Narasimham Committee on the Financial System

1. The committee's approach to financial sector reform is to ensure that the financial services industry operates on the basis of operational flexibility and functional autonomy with a view to enhance efficiency, productivity and profitability. A vibrant and competitive financial system alone will be able to sustain the ongoing structural reforms of the real sector economy.
2. One major factor responsible for depressed income of banks identified by the committee is the system of directed investment in terms of the SLR requirements and the relatively low rate of interest paid/received on these investments. Accordingly, the committee has recommended that the SLR should be brought down in a phased manner to 25 per cent (the minimum prescribed under the law) over a period of about five years. In the budget proposals for the year 1992-93, the SLR for incremental net demand and time liabilities of banks has

been reduced from 38.5 per cent to 30 per cent. This reduced the effective average SLR to 36 per cent during 1992-93. Some of the committee's points in respect of the rates of interest on SLR investments need to be controverted. First, these rates have been steadily revised upward in recent years. If a rise in the rate means higher interest return on new issues of government securities (bonds), it also inflicts capital losses on the holdings of old dated with lower coupon rates. As a policy option, it is much better for the authorities to try their level best to control the forces of inflation with a view to bring the rate of inflation down to a manageable level. By reigning in inflationary price expectation, it will make further rise in money rates of interest totally unnecessary. On the contrary, some lowering of the money rates of interest will become necessary. Therefore, in the context of continued success in keeping the forces of inflation under firm control, the current coupon rates on the recent issues of government bonds will become quite attractive to banks.

3. The committee has rightly pointed out that, at present, the CRR for the banks is much too high. In fact, since July 1, 1989 it had been pitched at its statutory maximum of 15 per cent of the net demand and time liabilities of banks. The RBI's justification for such a high CRR has been its perceived need for keeping the growth of money supply in the economy under control, in the face of much deficit spending by the government, resulting in excess increases year after year. With the government's attempt to reduce its fiscal deficit, the committee has recommended progressive reduction in the CRR from its present high level. It has also said that with the deregulation of interest rates, there would be more scope for the use of open market operations as a monetary control instrument by the RBI. Consequently, there would be less dependence on variations in CRR as a measure of monetary control.

   In addition, the committee has recommended that the interest rate paid to banks on their impounded reserves (under the CRR) above the basic minimum (of 3 per cent) should be increased: it should be broadly related to bank's average cost of deposits. It has added that, during the present regime of administered interest rates, this rate may be fixed at the level of bank's one-year deposit rate.

4. The most debatable recommendation of the committee is that for scaling down the priority sector credit from the present high level of 40 per cent of aggregate credit to 10 per cent. The committee admits that such directed credit has contributed much to the growth of a agriculture and small industry. But, it is of the view that such programmes should be re-examined at least in respect of those who are able to stand on their own feet and to whom these programmes with an element of concessionality in their rate of interest charged has become a source of economic rent.

   In view of the above, the committee has recommended that the directed credit programmes should be phased out. Recognising the need for their continuation for some time, it has recommended the following revised programme:

   a) The priority sector should be redefined to comprise the small and marginal farmer, the tiny sector of small industry, small business and transport operators, village and cottage industries, rural artisans and other weaker section

   b) The credit target for this redefined priority sector should now be fixed at 10 per cent of aggregate credit, which would be broadly in line with the credit flows to these sectors at present. (The committee has proposed that a review may be undertaken at the end of three years to see if directed credit programmes need to be continued.)

   c) As regards medium and large farmers, and the larger among small industries, including transport operators, etc., the committee has recommended that the RBI and other refinancing agencies should give preferential refinance to banks to encourage them to provide credit to the fore-mentioned sectors who would not constitute a part of the redefined priority sector.

5. The committee has recommended further deregulation of interest rates to reflect emerging market conditions.

However, for this, a reasonable degree of macro-economic balance through sufficient reduction in the fiscal deficit is necessary. Meanwhile, concessional interest rates should be phased out. Interest rates on bank deposits and the spread between the key rates may continue to be regulated by the RBI.

6. Banks (and financial institutions) in India suffer from capital inadequacy in relation to their risk-weighted assets. This should be removed within the next three years.

   The banks whose operations have been profitable and which enjoy a good reputation in the market should raise fresh capital from the public through the capital market. In respect of other banks, the government should meet the shortfall in their capital requirements by direct subscription to capital or by providing a loan that should be treated as subordinate debt.

7. Two very important recommendations of the committee concern the system of income accounting and loss provisioning followed by banks and other financial institutions in India. The committee has strongly recommended that the balance sheets (and income statements) of these institutions should be made transparent with full disclosures made in them according to international accounting standards. In regard to income recognition, the committee has recommended that the institutions following the accrual system of accounting should not recognise any income in their accounts in respect of "non-performing assets". They are defined as assets on which interest remains due for a period exceeding 180 days on the balance sheet date.

   For the purpose of provisioning, the committee has recommended that the assets of banks and other financial institutions should be classified into four categories, namely, standard, substandard, doubtful and loss assets and their provisioning should be done accordingly.

8. Banks at present experience considerable difficulties in recoveries of loans and enforcement of security charged to them. The committee, therefore, has recommended

strongly the setting up of special tribunals to speed up the process of recovery.

9. A novel recommendation of the committee is the establishment of a new financial institution called the Assets Reconstruction Fund (ARF), which would take over from banks and financial institutions a portion of their bad and doubtful debts at a discount, and subsequently follow up on the recovery of the dues owed to them from the primary borrowers. The fund would pay for the acquisition of these (bad and doubtful) assets from banks/DFIs at a discounted price (based on the realisable value of assets) in the form of five-year bonds which would bear interest at market-related rates and which would be guaranteed by the central government and thus would qualify as SLR assets.
10. The committee has made some suggestions (not operational recommendations) about the reorganisation of the structure of the banking system and of rural credit. (The suggestions have not been well-worked out moreover, they are not fully consistent with the committee's overall emphasis on the deregulation of the financial system.)
11. The committee has proposed that the government should indicate that there would be no further nationalisation of banks, that new banks in the private sector would be welcome subject to the normal requirements of the RBI, that branch licensing should be abolished and that the policy towards foreign banks should be made more liberal.
12. The committee has said that the internal organisation of banks is best left to the judgement of the management of individual banks, and that they should be free to make their own recruitment of officers, instead of having a common recruitment system with other banks except at the clerical level. The committee has stressed the need for a radical change in work technology and culture and greater flexibility in personnel policy. It has favoured computerisation.
13. In the committee's judgement, the Indian banking system, at present, is over-regulated and over-administered.

Instead, supervision should be based on prudential norms and regulations, with greater emphasis on internal audit and inspection.

14. The committee was firmly opposed to the duality of control over the banking system by the RBI and the banking division of the ministry of finance. Ending this, the RBI should be made the primary agency for the regulation of the banking system. Going a step further, the committee has recommended that a separate authority should be set up under the aegis of the RBI for the supervisory function over banks and DFIs (an unnecessary creation of yet another agency in our view).

11

SEBI and Capital Market Reforms

SEBI

The establishment of the Securities and Exchange Board of India (SEBI) was a significant government measure to monitor and regulate capital market activities and to promote healthy development of the market.

The SEBI was constituted in 1988 by a resolution of Government of India and it was made a statuary body by the Securities and Exchange Board of India Act, 1992.

Management

Section 4 of the Act lays down the constitution of SEBI — a chairman, two members from amongst the officials of the ministers of the central government dealing with finance and law, one member from amongst the officials of the Reserve Bank of India, two other members to be appointed by the central government, who shall be professionals and inter alia have experience or special knowledge relating to securities market.

The Act empowers the central government to supersede SEBI, if on account of grave emergency, SEBI is unable to discharge the functions and duties under any provisions of the Act, or SEBI persistently defaults in complying with any direction issued by the central government under the Act, or in the discharge of its functions and duties under the Act and as a result of such default the financial position of SEBI or its administration has deteriorated, or in public interest.

Objectives

According to the Act, the objectives of SEBI are to protect the interests of investors in securities and to promote the development of and to regulate, the securities market for matters connected therewith or incidental therewith.

Powers and Functions

The SEBI Act casts upon SEBI the duty to protect the interests of investors in securities market through appropriate measures, these measures provide for:

1. Regulating the business in stock exchanges and any other securities market.
2. Registering and regulating the working of stocks brokers, sub-broker, share transfer agents, bankers to an issue, trustees of trust deeds, registrars to an issue, merchant bankers, underwriters, portfolio managers, investment advisers and such other intermediaries who may be associated with security marketing in any manner.
3. Registering and regulating the working of collective investment schemes, including mutual funds.
4. Promoting and regulating self-regulating organisations.
5. Prohibiting fraudulent and unfair trade practices in securities market.
6. Promoting investor education and training of intermediaries in securities market.
7. Prohibiting insider trading in securities.
8. Regulating substantial acquisition of shares and takeover of companies.
9. Calling for information from, undertaking inspection, conducting enquiries and audits of the stock exchanges and intermediaries and self-regulatory organisations in the securities market.
10. Performing such functions and exercising such powers under the provisions of the Capital Issues (Control) Act, 1947 (subsequently repealed) and the Securities Contracts

(Regulation) Act, 1956, as may be delegated to it by the central government.

11. Levying fees or other charges for carrying out the purposes of section 11 of the Act.
12. Conducting research for the above purpose.
13. Performing such other functions as may be prescribed by the government.

The board may, for the protection of investors, specify, by regulations, the matters relating to issue of capital, transfer of securities and other matters incidental thereto and the manner in which such matters, shall be disclosed by the companies.

The SEBI is also empowered to issues such directions as may be appropriate to certain person or class of persons or company, intermediary or other persons referred to in section 12 (stock broker, sub-broker, share transfer agent, banker to an issue, trustee of trust deed, merchant banker, underwriter, registrar to an issue, investment adviser, portfolio manager, etc.): (a) In the interest of investors, or orderly development of securities market; or (b) to prevent the affairs of any intermediary or other persons referred to in section 12, being conducted in a manner detrimental to the interests of investors or securities market; or (c) to secure the management of any such intermediary or person.

Capital Market Reforms and Developments

The number of stock exchanges has increased and the capital market has expanded substantially. However, the functioning of the stock exchanges were characterised by many shortcomings with long delays, lack of transparency in procedures and vulnerability to price rigging and insider trading. A number of measures have been taken to overcome these problems. The objectives of these measures, broadly, have been to:

— Provide for effective control of the stock exchange operations.

— Increase the information flow and disclosures so as to enhance the transparency.

— Protect the interest of investors.

— Check insider trading.

— Improve the operational efficiency of the stock exchanges.
— Promote healthy development of the capital market.

Important measures of reform and development include the following:

Free Pricing

Raising of capital from the securities market before 1992 was regulated under the Capital Issues (Control) Act, 1947, which required companies to obtain approval from the Controller of Capital Issues (CCI) for raising resources in the market. New companies were allowed to issue shares only at par. Only the existing companies with substantial reserves could issue shares at a premium, which was based on some prescribed formula. In 1992, the Capital Issues (Control) Act 1947 was repealed and with this ended all controls relating to raising of resources from the market. Since then the issuers of securities could raise the capital from the market without requiring any consent from any authority either for making the issue or for pricing it. Restrictions on rights and bonus issues according to their assessment of market conditions have been removed.

Introduction of Book Building

To overcome the problem of determining the right price at which the market would clear an issue, the book building mechanism, was introduced in 1995. The book building mechanism is a method through which an offer price of an initial public offering (IPO) is based on investors' demand. The introduction of book building mechanism gave the issuer the choice to raise resources either through this or through the fixed price mechanism. The book building mechanism of floating new capital issues has been devised in such a way that small investors are also able to purchase securities at a price arrived through a transparent process. As the book building process is both time and cost-effective, it is becoming quite popular.

Electronic Trading

Till recently, trading on the Indian stock exchanges took place through open outcry system barring NSE and OTCEI, which adopted screen-based trading system from the beginning. At present all other stock exchanges have adopted online screen-based electronic trading, replacing the open outcry system. There are three main advantages of electronic trading over floor–based trading as observed in India, viz., transparency, more efficient price discovery, and reduction in transaction costs. Transparency ensures that stock prices fully reflect available information and lowers the trading costs by enabling the investor to assess overall supply and demand. Owing to computer–based trading, the speed with which new information gets reflected in prices has increased tremendously. The quantity and quality of information provided to market participants during the trading process (pre trading and post-trading) having significant bearing on the price formation has also improved.

Instruments and Market Participants

The capital market has widened and deepened considerably in the recent years with enlargement of participants and emergence of new instruments. In the Indian capital market, traditionally mainly two instruments were traded, i.e., debt and equity. However, starting from the mid-eighties and especially during the first-half of the nineties, a wide range of innovative/hybrid instruments combining both the features of debt and equity were introduced to suit varied needs of investors and issuers/ borrowers.

Market has also widened with the increase in the number of players, such as, mutual funds and foreign institutional investors.

Improvements in Trading, Clearing and Settlement Systems

The trading, clearing and settlement systems, which had suffered from several bottlenecks, have been considerably improved with measures taken to shorten the settlement cycle through the introduction of rolling settlement system and acceleration of the process of electronic book entry transfer through depository.

Increased Dematerialisation

Safe and quick transfer of securities is an important element for smooth and efficient functioning of the securities market. Apart from the problems involved in the movement of physical security certificates, bad deliveries due to faulty paper work, theft, forgery, etc., added to the transaction cost and restricted liquidity. To overcome these difficulties, legislative changes were carried out for maintaining ownership records in an electronic book-entry form. Under this mode, securities are transferred in a speedy and safe manner without interposition of issuers in the process. In order to catalyse the process of dematerialisation of securities and dematerialised trading, an element of compulsion was introduced by requiring the individual and institutional investors to settle trades compulsorily in dematerialised form in shares of selected companies.

Near Elimination of Counter-party Risk

One of the shortcomings of the clearing and settlement process of the Indian stock markets was the absence of a system to reduce counter-party risk. Managing this risk is essential for promoting a safe and efficient market. To provide the necessary funds and ensure timely completion of settlements in cases of failure of member brokers to fulfill their settlement obligations, major stock exchanges have set up settlement guarantee funds. The aggregate corpus of the fund at the stock exchange is presently over Rs.1,000 crores. The NSE has set up a clearing corporation that guarantees settlement of all trades. The clearing corporation, thus, assumes the counter party risk involved in all the transactions.

Circuit Breakers/Price Bands

Circuit breakers were first introduced in 1987 in the U.S. in the wake of a sharp fall in the share prices. To contain abnormal price variations, scrip–wise specific daily price bands or circuits breakers in India were introduced in 1995 whereby the trading automatically got suspended if the prices varied either side beyond 8 per cent; further trading was allowed only up to the price band.

It has been seen that circuit filters were successful in slowing down the market momentum. There has been some controversy over the effectiveness of circuit filters, as they could have adverse effects on the process of price formation. They are favoured mainly on the ground that they are the best available tool for containing volatility. This is based on the belief that containing of excess volatility helps to maintain investor confidence in the market.

Structure of Informational Flows

Several measures have been taken to enhance the transparency of the companies. A company offering securities in the Indian capital market is required to make a public disclosure of all relevant information through its offer documents, as indicated earlier. After a security is issued to the public and subsequently listed on a stock exchange, the stock exchange requires the issuing company to make continuing disclosure under the listing agreement. In India, all listed companies are now required to furnish to the stock exchanges and also publish mandated unaudited financial results on a quarterly basis.

Emphasis on Fair Trading Practices

Insider trading has been made a criminal offence punishable in accordance with the provisions under the SEBI Act, 1992. The regulations define an insider as a person who has access to price sensitive non-public information with regard to a company under the regulations. There are now separate regulations in place governing substantial acquisition of shares and takeover of companies. The regulations are aimed at making the takeover process more transparent and to protect the interests of minority shareholders.

Increasing Integration of Various Segments of Securities Markets

In India, different stock exchanges have so far followed their own practices relating to settlement producers creating segmentation of the market. While stock exchanges continue to follow different systems, certain developments have resulted in their better integration of the various segments of the Indian securities market. The two major stock exchanges, viz., BSE and NSE, have expanded their operations in different locations, thus, providing investors across the country with the facility to trade in the stocks listed/permitted in these stock exchanges. The inter–connected Stock Exchange of India Ltd. (ICSI) has been set up as an inter-connected market system and provides its trading members a facility to trade on the national market in addition to the trading facility at the regional stock exchanges.

12

Inflation and Monetary Policy

Meaning and Concept

Inflation has been defined as the persistent increase in the price level. Inflation has basically occupied the seat of paramount importance in the concept of macroeconomics. It is considered in terms of its impact and causes. One is the monetarists view and other is that of non-monetarists. The monetarists believe that inflation is a monetary phenomenon resulting from imbalance created between forces of demand and supply. However the non-monetarists state that inflation is a very complex phenomenon resulting from a number of social, political, economic factors and not only through the forces of demand and supply.

There are two types of inflation : demand-pull inflation and cost-push inflation. Demand-pull inflation is, when more money chases less quantity of goods and services, the excess demand relative to supply pushes up the prices of goods and services. However, if production cannot increase to neutralise the influence in monetary expenditure, then inflation may be serious. Often the demand-pull inflation precedes the cost-push inflation. When the former sets in there is an increasing demand for factors of production, prices of these also rise, leading to a hike in general prices. At times, cost-push inflation may also be independent of a rise in expenditure levels. It may be wage push (when wage earners are successful in bargaining for higher wages which are not linked with a rise in real productivity). In India, there is not much evidence of cost-push inflation, the major source of inflation has been from demand-pull.

Sharp and persistent increase in the price level over the decades has culminated into inflation, which is one of the major issues faced by Indian economy today. Due to this Budget 2007-

08 has emphasised on reducing the inflation levels from 6 per cent to 4 per cent.

Initially, prices started rising in India during and after the period of the World War. Soon the upheaval of partition added to this trend, and with minor fluctuations, the prices kept on rising in 1973, when the world oil crisis and consequent rise prices of imported oil brought in real inflationary trends in India.

Causes of Inflation

Inflation takes place when aggregate demand increases than aggregate supply or when cost increases. The causes of inflation are thus classified in two parts.

A. Demand side causes

B. Supply side causes.

A. Demand Side Causes

The following factors raise the demand:

i) *Increase in Money Supply.* The higher the growth rate of nominal money supply, the higher is the rate of inflation. The modern quantity theorists do not believe that true inflation starts after full employment. To support the same we can observe that all advanced countries have faced higher levels of unemployment and high rates of inflation.

ii) *Increase in Disposable Income.* Increase in disposable income increases people's demand for goods and services. The disposable income may increase with the rise in national income or reduction in taxes or reduction in the saving of people.

iii) *Increase in Consumer Spending.* The demand for goods and services increases when consumer expenditure increases. The reasons for high consumer spending could be due to conspicuous consumption or demonstration effect. Credit facilities to buy goods on hire purchase and instalment basis can also be one of the reasons of high spending.

iv) *Increase in Public Expenditure.* Expansion in government activities has resulted into increases government expenditure, thereby increasing the aggregate demand for goods and services. Government is providing more facilities through public utilities and social services and also starting public enterprises with the result that they help in increasing the aggregate demand.

v) *Cheap Monetary Policy.* The policy of credit expansion leads to increase in money supply, which in turn raises the aggregate demand for goods and services. This is known as credit-induced inflation.

vi) *Deficit Financing.* In order to meet its mounting expenses, the government resorts to deficit financing by borrowing from public and even by printing more currency notes. This in turn raises the aggregate demand in relation to the aggregate supply.

vii) *Black Money.* The existence of black money in all countries due to corruption and tax evasion increases the aggregate demand. People spend extravagantly on commodities as well as luxurious items to use this surplus money.

viii) *Expansion of the Private Sector.* Huge investments increase employment and income, thus, resulting into more demand for goods and services. However it takes time for the output to enter into market.

ix) *Repayment of Public Debt to the Public.* Repayment of past internal debt by government to the public increases the money supply, which tends to increase the aggregate demand for goods and services.

B. Supply Side Causes

The following factors tend to reduce the supply:

i) *Shortage of Factors of Production:* Shortage of factors like labor, raw materials, power supply, and capital leads to excess capacity and reduction in industrial production.

ii) *Natural Calamities.* Droughts and floods do affect the supplies of agricultural products resulting in shortages and thus increases inflationary pressures.

iii) *Artificial Scarcities.* This is created by hoarders and speculators who indulge in black marketing.

iv) *Increase in Exports.* When the country produces more goods for exports; it creates shortages in the domestic market.

v) *Industrial Disputes.* Countries having powerful trade unions also face shortages in supply. Trade unions resort to strikes, lockouts thus reducing the production level.

vi) *Law of Diminishing Returns.* If industries in the country use old machines and outmoded methods of production, this in turn raises the cost per unit of production.

vii) *International Factors.* Inflation is a worldwide problem. When prices rise in major industrial countries, its effects spread to all most all countries with which they have trade relations.

Control of Inflation (Anti-Inflationary Measures)
Monetary Policy

With the introduction of five-year plans, the need for adjustment in monetary and fiscal policies to suit the pace and pattern of planned development became imperative. The monetary policy since 1952 emphasized the twin aims of the economic policy of the government:

1. Speed up economic development in the country to raise national income and standard of living, and
2. Rreduce and control inflationary pressure in the economy.

This policy of the Reserve Bank of India since the first plan period was termed broadly as one of controlled expansion, i.e., a policy of "adequate financing of economic growth and at the same time ensuring reasonable price stability." Expansion of currency and credit was essential to meet the increased demand for investment funds in an economy like India that had embarked on rapid economic development. RBI recognised and appreciated the need for expansion of credit and money supply commensurate with the rapid development and diversification of the economy. Accordingly, the RBI helped the economy to expand via expansion of money and credit, and attempted to check rise in prices by the use of selective controls.

Objectives of Monetary Policy

The objectives of monetary policy change from time to time with the changes in the business activities and the level of economic development. Following are the main objectives of the monetary policy:

Growth with Stability

The most important objective of the developing countries is the maximisation of growth rate and stability of economy. Here, monetary policy plays a crucial role to mobilise resources in the private sector and their proper allocation. In developing countries, the maxim of monetary policy is controlled expansion of money supply. The supply of money has to be expanded in view of the requirements of growth and safeguards must be provided against over issue of currency resulting in uncontrolled inflation. The investment activities need to be boosted for achieving a high level of economic achievement. The monetary policy cannot only promote investment, it can also discourage investment in less productive and less useful activities. Thus, cheap and tight monetary measures can be adopted to encourage or discourage investment respectively, according to the requirement of business activities.

Price Stability

Price stability is the prime objective of the monetary policy in a developing country. Violent and frequent fluctuations in the internal price level, on one hand, disrupt the smooth functioning of the economy. On the other hand, it may also lead to insecurity and injustice. Inflation creates hardships to some sections of society, particularly, fixed income earners, while deflation plays havoc to almost everyone. Further, the effects of price instability are cumulative. Hence, the monetary authority should adopt a monetary policy in such a manner that helps in stabilising prices over a long period of time. If this happen, the development activities will go uninterrupted.

Exchange Rate Stability

International trade transactions take place on the basis of a fixed rate of exchange. Every country, which is the member of the International Monetary Fund, is committed to keep its exchange rate fixed at it's declared parity. It can be changed only to correct a fundamental disequilibrium. Any change in the equilibrium rate of exchange will have deep repercussion on the balance of payments of a country. The developing countries, being in the initial stage of development, have to import a wide range of capital goods and technical know-how to support their development programmes. As a result, their imports exceed exports and the balance of payment goes unfavourable. Therefore, monetary policy should be directed towards maintaining stability in the exchange rates and removing disequilibrium in the balance of payments.

Full Employment

It may not be very difficult for most of the countries to achieve the level of full employment, but the real problem is how to maintain it in the long period. Periodical fluctuations in the business activities may result in the unemployment in the economic system. If government wants to live up to the expectations of the people, the monetary authorities must ensure a high and stable level of employment. For the purpose, the current investment should be increased to exceed current savings through creation of credit or by higher velocity of circulation. When full employment is achieved, efforts should be made to equalise savings and investments.

LIMITATIONS OF THE MONETARY POLICY

The monetary policy plays an important role in the development of the developing countries. It is impersonal and indiscriminatory and involves least state interference in economic activities. Further, it has flexibility in operation and can be quickly applied, as the economic conditions change. The monetary policy can be easily adopted, modified or reversed in a short span of time, free from political pressure. However, the success of the monetary policy is limited by the following factors:

Underdeveloped Capital Market

The central bank cannot effectively implement the various credit control measures in the absence of well-developed and organised money as well as capital markets. However, most of the developing countries do not have such developed markets.

Unorganised Sector

In the developing countries, a sizeable part of financial resources come from the unorganised sector. As a result, the central bank fails to influence the market rate of interest by changing the bank rate.

Banking Habits of People

In developing countries, people do not understand the importance of banking institutions due to illiteracy, superstition and other social evils. People do not use credit instruments very often to perform their transactions. Further, due to the low level of income of people, most of the transactions are conducted with the help of money. Therefore, the credit control measures of the central bank fail to bring about the desired effects on the business activities.

Lack of Cooperation by the Banks

The success of the monetary policy depends on the cooperation extended by the commercial banks. In the developing countries, the commercial banks do not provide sufficient assistance to the central bank in implementing the monetary policy. Without proper coordination between the two, the monetary policy cannot succeed.

To overcome these limitations, the monetary authority must create conditions conducive to the growth of banking and financial institutions. Further, it should manipulate the monetary policy so as to step up saving and investment activities for accelerating the growth rate of the economy. The monetary authority must also exercise restrictions and controls.

MONETARY REGULATION IN INDIA

Before the establishment of RBI, the central government was responsible for the issue of the currency, while the credit control function was entrusted to the Imperial Bank of India. Now, the Reserve Bank is expected to organise currency and credit so that it fulfils the broad economic objectives of the country. The monetary policy since 1951 was supposed to fulfil twin objectives of the economic policy of the government, i.e. the rapid economic development and control of inflationary pressure generated in the economy as a result of vast development expenditure.

Monetary policy influences the economic trends, especially inventory investment through varying the cost and availability of the credit. The Reserve Bank administers the monetary policy by adopting various methods of credit control. Through these tools, the RBI influences the rate of interest (cost of credit), the supply of money and the access to or demand of money. These weapons of control are broadly classified into two: Quantitative and Qualitative controls.

Quantitative Controls

Quantitative controls are used to control the volume of credit and indirectly, to control the inflationary and deflationary pressures caused by expansion and contraction of credit. Quantitative controls are also known as General Credit Controls and consists of bank rate policy, open market operations and cash reserve ratio.

1. *Bank Rate:* The bank rate or central banks' discount rate is an important monetary instrument in modern economics. If monetary policy is effective and credible, a change in the bank rate will result in prime lending rate of banks and thus act as an independent instrument of monetary control. However, the role of the bank rate as an instrument of monetary policy has been very limited in India because of basic factors:

   — The structure of interest rates is administered by RBI— they are not automatically linked to the bank rate.

   — Commercial banks enjoy specific refinance facilities, and not necessarily rediscount their eligible securities with RBI at bank rate.

   — The bill market is underdeveloped and the different sub-markets of the money market are not influenced by the bank rate.

In other words, the bank rate in India is not the "pacesetter" to the other market rates of interest and the money market rates do not automatically adjust them to change in the bank rate.

2. *Cash Reserve Ratio (CRR) Requirements*: Another weapon available to RBI for credit control is the use of variable cash reserve requirements. Under the RBI Act, 1934, every commercial bank has to keep certain minimum cash reserves with RBI- initially; it was 5 per cent against demand deposits and 2 per cent against time deposits- these are known as Statutory Cash Reserves.

   Since Indian economy was passing through a severe liquidity problem since 1995-96 which adversely effected investment and production. The purpose of reducing CRR is to leave cash reserves with banks so as to enable them to expand bank credit.

3. *Statutory Liquidity Requirements:* Apart from cash reserve requirements, which commercial banks have to keep with RBI, all commercial banks have to maintain liquid assets in the form of gold, cash and unencumbered securities equal to not less than 25 per cent of their total demand and time deposit liabilities. Maintenance of liquid assets is a principle of sound banking.
4. *Open Market Operations:* In economics with well developed money markets, central banks use open market operations, i.e., buying and selling eligible securities by the central bank in the money market—to influence the volume of cash reserves with commercial banks and thus influence the volume of loans and advances they make to the industrial and commercial sectors. RBI had not used this weapon for many years. Open market operations control the credit creation power of the commercial banks in inflationary as well as deflationary situations in the economy. If the economy is faced with inflationary pressures, the central bank will sell securities in its possession. A reduction in cash reserves with the banks will reduce their credit creation capacity. Similarly, the central bank will offer to purchase the securities during deflationary conditions in the economy. In this process, the cash balances with the bank will rise.

Qualitative Controls

Qualitative methods of credit control are not adequate for effective control of credit supply. These methods have to be combined with qualitative methods. Qualitative methods of credit control are different from quantitative methods in the sense that they are directed towards particular uses of credit. Under the qualitative control methods, only non-essential uses are brought under the scope of central bank controls. The following are the important qualitative credit control methods:

1. *Margin Requirements:* The margin requirements are determined and changed by the central bank to influence the flow of credit against specific goods. Accordingly,

commercial banks may be required to fix lower or higher margins. When banks are asked to keep, say 60 per cent margin, then they can lend up to 40 per cent of the value of the security. When the margin is raised to 100 per cent, they can practically lend nothing. The instrument of margin requirements can be used not only to check speculative activities in the stock exchanges, but also in the commodity markets. When central bank desires more lendings against a particular security, it can lower margin requirements and vice versa.

2. *Rationing of Credit:* Under this method, the central bank fixes the ceiling of loans and advances. In certain cases, it may even fix the ceiling for specific categories of advances. When the central bank fixes a ceiling or maximum amount of loans for each commercial bank, it is known as variable portfolio ceiling. On the other hand, when the central bank fixes the ratio, which the capital of the commercial banks should have, to the total assets of the banks or any category of assets, it is known as Variable Capital Assets Ratio. The rationing of credit is a popular and a useful method of credit control in a planned economy in diverting resources into the channels fixed by the planning authorities. However, it will limit the freedom and initiative of banks severely. Therefore, credit rationing should be used as a temporary measure and that too under special circumstances.
3. *Regulation of Consumer Credit:* The regulation of consumer credit may involve controlling the total amount of credit for purchasing a particular durable good or regulating the time for repaying the debt. The central bank can reduce the flow of consumer's credit during the boom period in two ways. It can prescribe stiffer terms to banks by directing them to reduce the number of instalments through which the credit will be repaid. It can also impose a ceiling on the amount of loan that can be extended for buying a specific commodity. The regulation of consumer credit has been found quite effective, but its application encounters numerous difficulties.
4. *Control through Directives*: This power has been enjoyed by the central bank in the post-war period either by statute or by mutual consent between central bank and the

commercial banks. The effectiveness of this method depends upon the prestige of the central bank. Directives may take the form of oral or written statements, appeals and warnings. In many instances, the directives may not be liked by the commercial banks, but these are, no doubt, effective.

5. *Moral Suasion:* Moral suasion implies persuasion and request made by the central bank to the bank to follow the monetary policy of the former. During the depression period, it may request the commercial banks to fix lower margins, to accept inferior types of securities, which they may not normally accept, so as to create conditions stimulating bank credit. On the contrary, during inflationary pressure in the economy, the central bank may persuade the banks to avoid frequent loans, particularly for financing speculative, unproductive and non-essential activities. The effectiveness of moral suasion depends upon a number of factors such as:

   — Prestige and personal authority of central bank affected by its technical means and statutory power.
   — Country's banking and credit structure.
   — The degree of cooperation between the central bank and the commercial banks.
   — Dependence of commercial banks on the central bank.

6. *Publicity:* The central banks in many countries pursue the policy of publicity by reporting on the condition prevailing in the money market. Through the media of publicity, they may issue warnings to the people and the commercial banks so that banks may formulate an appropriate credit policy. This method is less effective in the underdeveloped countries. Due to mass illiteracy, people are not in a position to understand the implications of this policy. Thus, this instrument should be used with moderation and discretion.

7. *Direct Action:* Direct action refers to all the controls and directions, which a central bank may enforce on the banks to regulate their lending policies. Direct action generally involves coercive measures against the erring commercial banks. These may include denial or restrictions on

rediscounting facilities, charging of penal interest rates, fixation of quantitative credit ceiling.

Comparison between Quantitative and Qualitative Controls

It is clear that while quantitative methods affect indiscriminately all sections of the society, qualitative methods have discriminatory effects. Qualitative control methods have now become useful complements of the traditional and more general instruments of quantitative control methods. These methods control the composition of credit, rather than the total volume of the credit. Qualitative methods have become very popular in the recent decades due to their inherent flexibility. These methods can be satisfactorily applied to those sectors of economy that are susceptible to extreme fluctuations. Here, quantitative methods will not serve the desired object. The dependence on monetary authorities on qualitative methods has increased over time as they add to the strength of the central bank by supporting the quantitative methods.

Quantitative Methods	*Qualitative Methods*
1. These methods influence the total volume of credit indiscriminately without differentiating non-essential uses of credit.	1. These methods influence the direction of credit and are discriminatory in nature in the sense that they differentiate between essential and non-essential uses of credit.
2. These methods are mostly indirect and impersonal. The monetary authority has to wait and watch after bringing about the change.	2. These methods are more direct and entail more responsibility on the commercial banks as well as central bank to keep a constant check on the working of the former.
3. These methods affect the lenders. The borrowers need not necessarily be affected.	3. These methods necessarily affect both the lenders as well as the borrowers.

The qualitative control methods have been developed and perfected under the inflationary situation in the economy. However, like quantitative methods, their applicability during the depression has opened the question, particularly in the under-developed economics. Thus, we observe that both the methods fail to stimulate credit and investment during a period of depression.

13

Budget—Revenues and Expenditures

Central Budget

The budget is an estimate of government expenditure and revenue for the ensuing financial year, presented to parliament usually by the finance minister. Occasionally, in times of financial crisis, interim budgets may be introduced later in the year to increase taxation, expenditures, etc. Every budget, for instance, gives three sets of figures:

1. Actual figures for preceding years.
2. Budget and revised figures for the current year.
3. Budget estimates for the following year.

An estimate of all anticipated revenue and expenditure of the union government for the ensuing financial year is laid before parliament on the last working day of February every year. This is known as the Annual Financial Statement or the Budget, and covers the central government's transactions of all kinds in and outside India during the year in which the statement is prepared.

All receipts and disbursements of the union government are kept under two separate headings, namely, the Consolidated Fund of India and the Public Account of India. All revenue received, loans raised and money received in repayment of loans by the union government form the Consolidated Fund. No money can be withdrawn from this fund except under the authority of an Act of parliament. All other receipts and disbursements, such as deposits, service funds and remittances go into the public account, which is not subject to the vote of parliament. To meet unforeseen needs not provided in the Annual Appropriation Act, a contingency fund of India has also been established under Article 267(1) of the Constitution.

The presentation of the Annual Financial Statement is followed by a general discussion on the budget in both the houses of parliament. The estimates of expenditure from the Consolidated Fund of India are then placed before the Lok Sabha in the form of demands for grants. Ordinarily, a separate demand is made for each ministry. All withdrawals of money from the Consolidated Fund are thereafter authorised by an Appropriation Act embodied in another Bill, which is passed as Finance Bill of the year.

The Structure of the Budget

The budget is divided, vertically, into revenue (receipts) and expenditure (disbursements). Horizontally, it is divided into revenue account or revenue budget and capital account or capital budget.

1. Revenue Budget

The revenue budget deals with receipts from taxation and from non-tax sources and expenditure met out of these sources.

Tax revenue comes broadly from three sources:

— Taxes on income and expenditure.

— Taxes on property and capital or property transactions.

— Taxes on commodities and services.

Non-tax revenue consists of:

— Currency and coinage

— Interest receipts and dividends.

— Other non-tax revenue.

Expenditure: Current expenditure or revenue expenditure is met out of current revenues. Revenue expenditure is on:

1. General administration services including police, judiciary, defence and collection of taxes.
2. Social and community services, such as education, medical and public health, labour and employment.

3. Economic services like agriculture, industries, transportation, trade, etc.

A. Taxation Revenues of the Central Government (Classification of Taxes)

Taxes on Income and Expenditure

There are two types of income taxes: personal income tax and corporation tax.

1. *Personal Income Tax:* It is levied on individual by the central government and the proceeds are shared between the centre and the states. The income tax does not fall on all people but only on those people who are better off. It is based on the principal of taxation- "ability to pay". The following rates of income are applicable now:

In Case of Individuals (Other than Women or Individuals who are of the Age of 65 Years or More)

S.No.	*Income*	*Rate of Income Tax (%)*
1.	Up to Rs.100,000	Nil
2.	Rs.100,000–Rs.150,000	10 % in excess of Rs.100,000
3.	Rs.150,000–Rs.250,000	5,000 + 20% of income in excess of Rs. 150,000
4.	Above Rs.250,000 excess of Rs.250,000	250,00 + 30% of income in

In Case of Women (Other than Women who are of the Age of 65 Years or More)

S.No.	*Income*	*Rate of Income Tax (%)*
1.	Up to Rs.135,000	Nil
2.	Rs.135,000–Rs.150,000	10 % in excess of Rs.135,000
3.	Rs.150,000–Rs.250,000	1500 + 20% of income in excess of Rs. 150,000
4.	Above Rs.250,000	21500 + 30% of income in excess of Rs.250,000

In case of individuals who are of the age of 65 years or more.

S.No.	*Income*	*Rate of Income Tax (%)*
1.	Up to Rs.185,000	Nil
2.	Rs.185000–Rs.250,000	20 % in excess of Rs.185,000
3.	Above Rs.250,000	13,500 + 30% of income in excess of Rs. 250,000

Income tax is progressive, i.e., the rate of tax is not uniform but rises progressively with the rise in money income.

2. *Corporation Tax:* It is a tax on the income of companies. Corporation tax is imposed by central government on the profits of large and small companies.

   Domestic company: 35 per cent of their net profit

   Foreign company: 40 per cent of their net profit

   In 1996-97, the government of India imposed the Minimum Alternate Tax (MAT) on companies, which escaped the corporate tax net by using the provisions of exemptions, deductions, incentives, differential rate of depreciation, etc.

3. *Interest Tax:* The Interest Tax Act 1974 provided for the levy and a special tax on the gross amount of interest accruing to the commercial banks on loans and advances made by them in India. The government withdrew this tax in 1985 but later reintroduced it as an anti- inflationary measure. The tax is levied on the gross interest income of 'credit institutions', that is, banks, public financial institutions, financial companies, etc. The interest tax paid by banks and financial institutions was abolished in the 2000-01 budget.

4. *Expenditure Tax:* The government imposed an expenditure tax under Expenditure Tax Act 1987. This act provides for levy of a tax on expenditure incurred in hotels where the room charges for any unit of residential accommodation are Rs. 400 or more per day per individual. The rates of this tax have been revised later from 10 per cent to 20 per cent and the tax was extended to expenditure incurred in restaurants providing superior facilities of air-conditioning, etc. The expenditure tax has now been phased out.

Raxes on Property and Capital Transactions

The central government has imposed certain taxes on wealth and capital transactions.

1. *Estate Duty:* Estate duty was imposed on the estate of a person that was inherited by his heirs. The duty was imposed and collected by the central government but the proceeds were passed on to the states. As the tax yield was too low and the administrative cost was too high, a sensible decision was taken to abolish it in March 1985.
2. *Gift Tax:* It was imposed in April 1958 as a complement to the estate duty, wealth tax and the expenditure tax as necessary to prevent evasion of the other three taxes. The gift tax is charged every financial year on gifts made during the previous year. It is imposed on the donor, and the rate was highly progressive according to the value of the gift. But, finally, the gift tax has been abolished on the ground of its ridiculously low yield.
3. *Wealth Tax:* This tax has been imposed on accumulated wealth or property of every individual, Hindu undivided family and closely held companies. With effect from April 1993, wealth tax is chargeable in respect of the net wealth exceeding Rs. 15 lakhs at the rate of 1 per cent. The original purpose of imposing taxes on property and on transfer of property was to reduce the growing inequalities of income and wealth. This purpose was never achieved because of high rates of wealth tax in the beginning, the various exemptions allowed over the years and the corrupt direct tax administration. These taxes should have been dropped long ago but no finance minister had the courage to drop it.

Taxes on Commodities and Services

Revenue from commodity taxation is the most important source of revenue for the central government.

1. *Central Excise Duties:* These duties are levied by the centre on commodities that are produced within the country. But commodities on which state government imposes excise duties are exempt from central excise duties. The central

government shares the proceeds of the central excise duty with the states according to the formulas determined by the finance commission. But under the recommendations of the Eleventh Finance Commission, there is no specific transfer of excise duties to the states.

2. *Service tax:* Besides excise duties, the Government of India is now imposing service tax on telephones, brokerages, insurance, etc. This tax has been widened over the years. It is one of the fastest growing taxes for the central government.
3. *Custom Duties:* These are duties or taxes imposed on commodities imported into India. Duties levied on goods or commodities exported from India are export duties. The government has removed export duties in order to promote it.

B. Non-tax Revenues of the Central Government

Besides taxes on income, property and commodities, the central government gets revenue from other sources also, which are collectively called Non-tax Revenue. These include receipts from fiscal services, interest receipts, dividends and profits of government enterprises, general services, etc.

Fiscal services relate to revenue received by the central government from:

— Currency and coinage, and

— Other fiscal services relating to Indian security press, Nasik, Hyderabad, etc.

General services include also social community services, economic services and grants-in-aid and contributions. Interest receipts which constitute the most important source of non-tax revenue comprising interest on loans to states and union territories, interest payable by railways, postal services, and other interest receipts. Profits and dividends relate to profits of RBI, profits of nationalised banks, LIC, public enterprises, etc.

Expenditure of the Central Government

There has been tremendous increase in the expenditure of the central government, particularly in revenue expenditure financed through current taxation and other current non-tax revenues.

Before 1987-88, the revenue expenditure of central government was broadly classified into three types:

1. Civil expenditure includes general services, social and community services and economic services.
2. Defence expenditure includes expenditure on armed forces, pensions given to the retired armed personnel, etc.
3. Other expenditure includes collection of taxes and duties, interest payments, grants to states, etc.

The central government adopted a new classification of public expenditure from the 1987-88 budget. Under this new classification, all public expenditure is classified into:

1. *Non-plan Expenditure:* The non-plan expenditure of central government is divided into revenue expenditure and capital expenditure. Revenue expenditure includes interest payments, defence revenue expenditure, subsidies, pension and other general services, economic services, grants to states and union territories and grants to foreign governments. Capital non-plan expenditure includes such items as: defence capital expenditure, loans to public enterprise, loans to states and union territories and loans to foreign government.
2. *Plan Expenditure:* It comprises:
   - — Central plans, such as on agriculture, rural development, irrigation and flood control, energy, industry and minerals, transport, communications, science and technology, environment, etc.
   - — Central assistance for plans of the states and union territories.

2. Capital Budget

Capital expenditure of the central government consists of plan expenditure and non-plan expenditure financed out of capital receipts.

The capital expenditure of the central government consists of:

1. Loans to states and union territories for financing plan projects, and loans to foreign governments.
2. Capital expenditure on economic development.

3. Capital expenditure on social and community development.
4. Capital expenditure on defence.
5. Capital expenditure on general services.

The capital receipts of central government comprises of:

1. Net recoveries of loans and advances to state governments and union territories and public sector enterprises.
2. Net market borrowings (i.e., gross borrowings less repayments).
3. Net small savings collections (gross small savings less states share).
4. Other capital receipts that include provident funds, special deposits, etc.

Importance of the Budget

There is no other government measure that affects the whole economy as the budget. No wonder all sections of the people await the annual budget with mixed feelings—anxiety, fear and hope. The endeavour of the finance minister is to present a budget that gives maximum support to forces that can move the country forward on the path of growth with stability and social justice.

The budget should set the stage for the achievement of economic and social goals.

In India, today, about half of the GDP is channelled into the government sector by the union, state and union territories' budgets and disbursed by the union, state and union territories governments under various developmental and non-developmental heads. These indicate the development and distributive importance and implications of the budgetary operations. There has been a steep increase in the government expenditures, both in absolute and relative terms. The total budgetary expenditures (of the centre, state and union territories) are about 50 per cent of the GDP today. The central government expenditure alone account for over one-fourth of the GDP.

In a developing economy like India, the budget policy has to serve the following purposes:

1. Accelerate the pace of economic development by mobilising resources for the public sector and their optimal allocation.
2. Affect improvement in production in the private sector in accordance with the national priorities.
3. Affect improvements in income distribution.
4. Promote exports and encourage import substitution.
5. Achieve economic stabilisation.

To serve these purposes, apart from the judicious allocation of the budgetary resources, various fiscal incentives and disincentives are also employed by the budget.

Tax Reforms — Kelkar Committee Report

The Finance ministry set up a task force under the chairmanship of Vijay Kelkar on the implementation of the Fiscal Responsibility and Budget Management (FRBM). The task force made recommendations to bring about a radical transformation of Indian tax system.

Philosophy of the Task Force

1. The task force disagreed with the existing approach of the government to reduce government expenditure to achieve fiscal consolidation. It has, instead favoured a revenue-led approach to be accomplished by raising revenues more than by compressing expenditure.
2. It further suggests that the government should enhance capital expenditure in order to counter-balance the contractionary effects of fiscal consolidation.
3. The report favoured revenue mobilisation through low and few tax rates alongside widening of tax base and shifting the incidence of taxation on consumption.
4. The task force has strongly favoured a Value-Added Tax (VAT) regime. The destination-based VAT on all goods and services is the best method of eliminating distortions and taxing consumptions. The task force states that it is always possible to pick sectors with easy enforceability – such as

telecom, banking or oil – and impose taxes on them. However, such an approach is not a long-term foundation for a sound tax system. Thus, the task force recommends a Goods and Services Tax (GST) across the board.

Recommendations of the Task Force

The task force, in order to bring about a radical transformation of the Indian tax system, has proposed radical changes in both direct taxes and indirect taxes.

I. Direct Taxes

1. For Income tax payers, the marginal rate of income tax would be nil up to Rs. 1 lakh. Only two slabs are proposed for the higher incomes: 10 per cent for income level of Rs. 1 lakhs to Rs.1.5 lakhs; 20 per cent for income level of Rs.1.5 lakhs to Rs. 2.5 lakhs and 30 per cent for incomes above Rs. 2.5 lakhs.
2. The standard deduction available to the salaried taxpayers will be done away with and all exemptions are abolished, except those relating to housing loans, senior citizens and women.
3. For corporates, the task force has proposed a reduction in the rate of corporation tax from 35.875 per cent to 30 per cent for domestic companies.
4. Depreciation rate has been lowered from 25 per cent to 15 per cent.
5. It has proposed to eliminate the tax on distribution of dividends, while preserving exemptions from the income tax of dividends in the hands of the recipient.

II. Indirect Taxes

1. The centre as well as the state should have concurrent power to levy Goods and Services Tax (GST). This would require a change in the constitution so that both the Centre and the state are authorised to levy GST.
2. The task force requires both the centre and the state, the number of tax rates proposed to be restricted to three ad-

valorem rates, in addition to zero rate. Under the proposal, the centre would have three rates – 6 per cent (floor), 12 per cent (standard) and 20 per cent (higher). Similarly, the states would have three rates – 4 per cent (floor), 8 per cent (standard) and 14 per cent (higher). The total burden on most goods and services works out to be 20 per cent – 12 per cent by the centre and 8 per cent by the states. The standard Central rate of 12 per cent, as proposed by the task force, is lower than the current CENVAT rate of 16 per cent.

3. The introduction of GST at the central and the state level should be accompanied by the withdrawal of all cascading taxes such as central sales tax, octroi duty, state level sales tax, entry tax, stamp duty, telecom licence fee, turnover tax, tax on consumption of electricity, taxation of transportation of goods and passengers.
4. Imports will be charged a two-part levy representing the central GST and the state GST. However, exports are zero-rated.
5. The task force makes an attempt for the proposed tax regime by seeking to exempt from VAT all small businesses, whether in manufacturing or services, with a turnover of up to Rs. 25 lakhs. This will certainly reduce the administrative burden in tracking small businesses.
6. The baseline projection of the task force show that the country's fiscal stress will increase under the present tax regime. They show that revenue deficit in 2008-09 will be 1.66 per cent of GDP and fiscal deficit will be 3.98 per cent of the GDP.

Appraisal of the Kelkar Committee Report

The proposal of the Task Force is considered very radical because they intend to transplant a new tax regime by overhauling the present tax regime.

To reduce the gap between the statutory and effective tax rate, the task force has recommended three measures – to reduce the general rate of depreciation from 25 per cent to 15 per cent and to abolish all tax incentives on new units and lower the corporate tax rate from 35.875 per cent to 30 per cent. The UPA government is making an effort to increase investment in rural infrastructure and backward states and backward areas. If all tax exemptions for new units set up in rural areas and backward states are to be abolished, it would be well impossible to attract private investment in such areas and thus, the total burden of developing rural infrastructure and backward areas will fall on the public sector. This would certainly go against the policy of expanding the role of the private sector along with that of the public sector in infrastructure development. Redressal of regional imbalances among states will also become difficult.

There are thousands of people who incur expenditure far in excess of the income disclosed in their income tax return. It has been alleged that tax administration in India has not been able to bring them into the tax net. Even though one-by-six filing of return scheme has been in operation for last nine years, very little success has been achieved in forcing the big spenders, but low income tax payers, to cough out more in the form of income tax. Among the large number of tax evaders can be included moneylenders in rural India, suppliers of construction materials such as cement, steel and bricks, traders in fertilisers and pesticides, shopkeepers and retailers, transport operators and truck operators and other businessmen. Although the Income Tax Act (1961) has been amended to tax the amount of expenditure where the assessee is not able to offer a satisfactory explanation, yet the actual realisation under this head is very little.

The central government has after a continuous effort extending over several years has been able to persuade the states to impose the Value-Added tax (VAT) with effect from 1 April 2005. This was on the basis of an assurance by the central government that in case the states lose revenue in the initial years, the central government will provide compensation. For this purpose, an expert committee is to be set up. The Kelkar Task Force intends to introduce goods and services tax (GST) with a 12 per cent rate of the central and 8 per cent rate in the states. There is no doubt that the Kelkar Task Force by its prescription of one-point taxation has presented a very simple system instead of a large number of taxes prevailing earlier, but what is the guarantee that GST will not be evaded.

VALUE ADDED TAX (VAT)
THE CONCEPT AND IMPLEMENTATION

A compulsory contribution to the support of the government levied on persons incomes, commodities, transactions, etc., is called a Tax. Earlier to VAT prevailed the Sales Tax System. It contained various weaknesses:

— *Deficiency relates to its cascading effect.* The sales tax is levied on the gross value without allowing any credit or set-off for the taxes paid on inputs.

— *Lacks transparency:* The existing system results in an uncontrolled incidence of the tax because the tax system lacks transparency.

— *There is the problem of multiplicity of rates:* Prior to the reforms in the sales tax system, a large number of rates slabs are still in existence under the present sales tax system.

— *Heterogeneity prevails in the structure of tax as well:* In addition to general sales tax, most states levy an additional sales tax, turnover tax or a surcharge.

— *Economic consequence of widespread taxation of input*: It led to vertical integration of firms, i.e., the existing systems of taxes militates against ancillary industries and encourages them to produce more and more of the inputs needed rather than purchase them from ancillary industries.

— *Lacks neutrality*: It interferes with the producers' choice of inputs and outputs as well as the consumers' choice for consumption, thereby leading to severe economic distortions.

Value Added Tax

In the existing structure before a commodity is produced, inputs are first taxed, and then, after the commodity is produced with input tax load output is taxed again. This causes an unfair double taxation with cascading effect. In VAT, a set-off will be given for input tax as well as on tax paid on previous purchases. Other taxes such as turnover tax, surcharge, additional surcharge, etc., will be abolished.

VAT, which is paid by any dealer in any quarter can be also be calculated as:

VAT= Tax Liability - Input Tax Credit

The question arises: what is input tax credit and what is tax liability? To understand it we will have to know the input tax.

Input Tax

All the things you buy locally will carry VAT charge. (i.e., Local tax would have been levied on it), but if you are a registered dealer, you can normally claim a credit for the VAT charged on most business purchases. This is your Input Tax. Input tax is the tax (local only) that you have paid to your supplier on your entire purchases made during the quarter under consideration.

Tax Liability

This is the tax (local and central sales tax) you would charge your customer on all your sales made during the quarter under consideration.

VAT provides various advantages such as:

- Overall tax burden will be rationalised, prices will in general fall.
- There will be self-assessment by dealers.
- Transparency will increase.
- There will be higher revenue growth.
- VAT will help common people, traders, industrialists and also the government.
- It is indeed a move towards more efficiency, equal competition and fairness in the taxation system.
- It prevents tax self-policing method and creates 'favourable' environment for honest businessman.

With so many benefits attached to VAT, one would wonder why VAT is not being implemented and accepted easily and immediately in India. The reasons are that one cannot implement the taxation system divided as one part to be VAT and the other to be the conventional taxation. The entire system has to be one and uniform. Secondly, presently the excise and custom fall under the central government and sales tax under state government, and each state government has its own rules, thus, no uniformity as such prevails in rates of tax. Therefore, VAT cannot be brought up immediately.

Besides, there are certain negative points in the VAT structure which reduces the chances of this tax to rise up.

1. VAT leads to inflation due to two factors:
   — It levies additional tax on distribution and profit element of intermediaries.
   — As a higher amount of tax is paid it involves more investment, which has its own cost.

Thus, VAT leads to inflation as it is paid in advance at stages leading to increased investment in business.

2. VAT involves big refunds, which is possible only due to positive mental state of the refunds arising due to state sale, exports, etc., and there is always a big time gap between the date of collection and an refund of tax. Hence it is an almost impossible condition to comply with.
3. VAT requires an accurate and comprehensive financial planning by the government to arrive at the retainable tax because there is always an involvement of refunds.
4. Risk of bogus as well as set off is very high on the basis of fake tax invoice.

Calculation of VAT

Primarily, there are two methods:

1) The Invoice or the Tax Credit method.
2) The Subtraction method.

Invoice method: The tax is calculated and separately charged on each sale and accordingly shown in the invoices. The difference between the tax payable on sale and the tax paid on purchase (as per the invoice) is VAT.

Subtraction method: The tax is calculated on the aggregate value of sales and purchases by applying the rate of tax as applicable to the goods. The difference between the tax on sale value and Purchase value is VAT.

To illustrate: The value of purchase is Rs. 100. The value of sales is Rs 150. VAT rate is 12.5 per cent.

As per invoice method:

Tax payable on sales (as per invoice)	18.75
Taxes paid on purchase (as per invoice)	12.5
VAT	Rs. 6.25

As per subtraction method:

Value of sales	150
Tax thereon (A)	18.75
Value of purchase	100
Tax thereon (B)	12.5
VAT [(A) – (B)]	Rs. 6.5

Effectively, VAT is on the price, which the consumer pays. It is collected in stages. The tax paid on earlier stage is allowed as 'credit' or 'set off'.

14

The Economic Content of Common Minimum Programme

Congress and its alliance parties—DMK, PMK, NCP, RJD, Lok Jana Shakti Party, PDP, JMM, IUML along with the leftist parties led by CPI (M), CPI Forward Bloc, etc.—have been working together to formulate a Common Minimum Programme (CMP). This group described as United Progressive Alliance (UPA) released the final draft of CMP on 27 May 2004.

Principles of CMP

1. To preserve, protect and promote social harmony.
2. To ensure that the economy grows at least 7-8 per cent per year in a sustained manner over a decade and more and in a manner that generates employment so that each family is assured a safe and viable livelihood.
3. To enhance the welfare and well-being of farmers, farm labour and workers, particularly those in the unorganised sector.
4. To fully empower women politically, educationally, economically and legally.
5. To provide for full equality of opportunity, particularly in education and employment for the Scheduled Castes, Scheduled Tribes, OBCs and religious minorities.
6. To unleash the creative energies of our entrepreneurs, businessmen, scientists, engineers and all other professionals and productive forces of society.

Initiatives Proposed by UPA Government

The UPA reiterates its abiding commitment to economic reforms which stimulates growth, investment and employment. Further reforms are needed and will be carried out in agriculture, industry and services. The UPA's economic reforms will be oriented primarily to spreading and deepening rural prosperity, to significantly improving the quality of public systems and delivery of public services to bring about a visible and tangible difference in the quality of life of ordinary citizens of the country.

The initiatives proposed by UPA government have been detailed in the CMP in the following manner.

a) Employment

To enact a National Employment Guarantee Act to provide for at least 100 days of employment, to begin with on asset, creating public works programmes every year at minimum wages for at least one able-bodied person in every rural, urban poor and middle class household.

b) Agriculture

To ensure that public investment in agricultural research extension, rural infrastructure and irrigation be stepped up in a significant manner. Irrigation will receive the highest priority, and all ongoing projects will be completed according to a strict time schedule.

The government will ensure that the flow of rural credit is doubled in the next three years, and that the coverage of the small and marginal farmers by institutional lending is expanded substantially.

The government will introduce a special programme for dry land farming in the arid and semi-arid regions of the country.

c) Education and Health

The UPA government pledges to raise public expenditure in education to at least 6 per cent of GDP with at least half of this amount being spent on primary and secondary schools. The government will introduce a cess on all central taxes to finance the commitment to universalise access to quality basic education. It will also ensure that nobody is denied of professional education because he or she is poor. The UPA government will raise public spending on health to at least 2 – 3 per cent of the GDP over the next five years.

d) Food and Nutrition Security

A comprehensive medium–term strategy for food and nutrition security will be worked out in the next three months with an objective of universal food security over time, if found feasible. The UPA government will strengthen the Public Distribution System (PDS), particularly in the poorest and the backward blocks of the country.

e) Scheduled Castes and Scheduled Tribes

The government will urge the states to make legislation for conferring ownership rights in respect of minor forest produce, including tendu patta, on all those people from the weaker sections who work in the forests.

All reservation quotas, including those related to promotions will be fulfilled in a time-bound manner.

f) Infrastructure

The UPA government attaches the highest priority to the development and expansion of physical infrastructure like roads, highways, ports, railways, water supply, sewerage treatment and sanitation. Public investment in infrastructure will be enhanced, even as the role of private sector is expanded. A comprehensive programme for urban renewal and massive expansion of social housing in towns and cities, paying particular attention to the needs of slum dwellers, will be taken into consideration.

g) Drinking Water

The acute drinking water shortage has become a big issue in cities. The CMP will consider on providing drinking water to all sections in urban and rural areas and augmenting the availability of drinking water resources. Harvesting rainwater, desalting existing ponds and other innovative mechanisms will be adopted.

h) Regional Development

The central government will also take proactive measures to speed up the industrialisation of eastern and north-eastern regions. It will consider the creation of a Backward States Grants Fund that will be used to create productive assets in backward states like Bihar, UP and Assam.

i) Foreign Direct Investment

The country needs at least two to three times the present level of FDI inflows. Therefore, FDI will continue to be encouraged and actively sought, particularly in areas of infrastructure, high technology and exports, and where local assets and employment are created on a significant scale.

j) Industry

Necessary steps are to taken to boost private investment. FDI will continue to be encouraged and actively sought, particularly, in the areas of infrastructure, high technology and exports and where local assets and employment are created on a significant scale. Indian industry will be given every support to become competitive. The government will set up the National Manufacturing Competitiveness Council to provide a continuing forum for policy dialogue to energise and sustain the growth of manufacturing industry. Household and artisanal manufacturing will be given greater technological, investment and marketing support.

k) SSI Sector

In the past few years, the most employment intensive sectors of small-scale industry have suffered extensively. A major promotional package for SSI sector will be coming up very soon.

l) Public Sector

The UPA government will retain the existing 'Navratna' companies in the public sector. These companies can raise resources from the capital market. Efforts will be made to modernise and restructure sick public sector companies and revive sick industry. All privatisation will be considered on a transparent basis and case-by-case basis. The government believes that privatisation should increase competition, not decrease it. It will not support the emergence of any monopoly that only restricts competition.

m) Labour

The UPA government is firmly committed to ensure the welfare and well being of all the workers, particularly those in the unorganised sector who constitute 93 per cent of our workforce. It recognises that some changes in labour laws may be required, but changes must fully protect the interests of workers and families and must take place after full consultation with trade unions.

n) Fiscal Policy

The government commits itself to eliminate the revenue deficit of the centre by 2009, so as to release more resources for investments in social and physical infrastructure. While reducing the deficit, the UPA government will not cut deficits by reducing or curtailing growth of investment and development outlays. Along with this, effective and strong measures will be taken to control price hike of essential commodities.

o) Capital Market

The government will ensure the orderly functioning of capital markets that reflect the true fundamentals of the economy. Financial markets will be deepened and FIIs will continue to be encouraged. Misuse of double taxation agreement will be stopped, interest of small investors will be protected and they will be given new avenues for safe investment of their savings. SEBI will be further strengthened.

p) Economic Reforms

The UPA's economic reforms will be oriented primarily to spreading and deepening rural prosperity, to significantly improving the quality of public systems and delivery of public services to bring about a visible and tangible difference in the quality of life of ordinary citizens of the country. The reforms will be carried out in agriculture, industry and services.

Comparison of Issues of UPA and NDA Government

The Common Minimum Programme formulated by the Congress with 14 other alliance partners is basically aimed at achieving growth with social and economic justice for the farmers, agricultural labour, unorganised sector and weaker sections of the society. There are basically the following issues in which the UPA dispensation differs sharply from the thinking of the NDA.

1. The UPA has categorically taken stand that public sector undertakings (PSUs) which are profit making will not be privatised and that economy needs a strong public sector along with the strong private sector.
2. The approach to labour policy has dealt a severe below to the demand for 'hire and fire' vigorously pursued by FICCI, ASSOCHAM and CII. Although rationalisation of labour laws has been conceded by the UPA, yet it has totally rejected the idea of 'automatic hire and fire'. Even in the present situation, when Chapter VB of the Industrial Disputes Act is very much in existence, the employers are using lockouts on an extensive scale to downsize labour.

To conclude, the Common Minimum Programme (CMP) is motivated by good intentions and promises to push forward economic reforms with a human face and providing corruption-free, transparent and accountable system of government.

15

Expenditure Policy — Pay Commission, Finance Commission

Finance Commission

— A finance commission is appointed every five years by the president, under Article 280, to determine:

  — The distribution of net proceeds of taxes to be shared between the centre and the states;

  — The principles that should govern the payments by union of grants in aid to states;

  — Any other matter concerning financial relations between the centre and states.

— Their recommendations are called awards.

— After 74th amendment, finance commission is required to recommend steps to supplement resources of local bodies also.

— Till date, 11 finance commissions have given their awards.

11TH Finance Commission

— Chairman: A.M.Khusro

— Submitted: interim report : January 15, 2000

— Final Report: July 7, 2000

— Supplementary Report : August 31, 2000

— First FC, which was mandated to recommend the measures, needed to augment the consolidated fund of the state to supplement the resources of the panchayats and municipalities.

Recommendations

— Twenty per cent of net revenue proceeds of shareable central taxes and duties should be transferred to the state.

— In addition to the above, 1.5 per cent of the net revenue should also be transferred to the sales by not imposing sales tax on sugar, tobacco and textiles.

— Upper limit of transferable revenue proceeds from the centre should not exceed by 37.5 per cent of the total revenue.

Weightage Formula

Population : 10%.

Deviation from average per capita income : 62.5%.

Area : 7.5%

Infrastructure Index : 7.5%

Tax effort : 5% and

Fiscal discipline : 7.5%

— Total grant-in-aid of Rs. 35,359 crore of states for solving the problem of revenue deficits. Out of this 85 per cent amount is to given to 15 identified states. The remaining amount of Rs. 5,303.86 crores should be transferred to Promotional Fund along with the same additional amount added by the central government. This amount is to be distributed among all the states on the basis of their fiscal performance during 2000-05.

— Grant-in-aid of Rs. 10,000 crore for local bodies during 2000-05 i.e. Rs. 2,000 crore every year (Rs.1,600 crore for rural bodies and Rs. 400 crore for urban bodies.)

— Repayment of specific debts given to Punjab in 1984-94 for removing terrorist activities should remain suspended up to 2005.

— Services should be brought under taxation and service tax be included in the concurrent list.

Suggestions

— To modify the limits of professional tax.

— To determine the rates of water and electricity charges on the basis of cost itself.

— To set up pay commission on the advice of states.

— For exploring the measures to reduce the burden of pension of the treasury.

12TH FINANCIAL COMMISSION

Chairman: Dr. C. Rangarajan.

Terms of Reference

— The commission will make recommendations on:

- — The distribution of the divisible pool of net proceeds of taxes between the union and the states and the allocation between the states of such proceeds.
- — Principles governing grants on aid of the revenues of the state out of the Consolidated Fund of India and grants under Article 275 of Constitution, and
- — The measures needed to augment the Consolidated Fund of a state to supplement the resources of the panchayats and municipalities.
- — In addition, the commission is also required to review the fiscal reforms facility introduced by the central government on the basis of the recommendation of the eleventh financial commission and suggest measures for effective achievement of its objectives.
- — The commission has been asked to submit its report by July 31, 2004, covering a period of five years commencing on April 1, 2005.

Recommendations

— The commission submitted its report on November 30, 2004 covering the period 2005-10. The recommendations of the commission include a plan for restructuring of public finances of the centre and the states through improvement in revenue mobilisation and bringing down debt levels, and through enactment of fiscal responsibility legislation of states. The commission recommended debt relief of states likes to fiscal reforms, doing away with the present system of central assistance to state plans in the form of grants and loans and transfer of external assistance to states on the same terms and conditions as attached to such assistance by external funding agencies.

— The TFC raised the share of states in shareable central taxes from 29.5 per cent to 30.5 per cent. Total transfers to States recommended by the TFC amount to Rs. 7,55,752 crore over the five-year period 2005-10. Of this, transfer by way of share in central taxes and grant-in-aid amount to Rs. 6,13,112 crore and Rs. 1,42,640 crore, respectively.

— The total transfers recommended by the TFC are higher by 73.8 per cent over those recommended by the Eleventh Financial Commission (EFC). Within the total transfers, while the share in central taxes is higher by 62.9 per cent, grants-in-aid recommended by TFC are higher by 143.5 per cent over those recommended by EFC.

Restructuring Public Finance

— Centre and states to improve the combined tax-GDP ratio to 17.6 per cent by 2009-10.

— Combined debt-GDP ratio, with external debt measured at historical exchange rates, to be brought down to 75 per cent by 2009-10.

— Fiscal deficit to GDP targets for the centre and states to be brought down to zero by 2008-09.

— Interest payments relative to revenue receipts to be brought down to 28 per cent and 15 per cent in the case of the Centre and States, respectively.

— States to follow a recruitment policy in a manner so that the total salary bill, relative to revenue expenditure, net of interest payments, does not exceed 35 per cent.

— Each state to enact a fiscal responsibility legislation providing for elimination of revenue deficit by 2008-09 and reducing fiscal deficit to 3 per cent of State Domestic Product.

— The system of on-lending to be brought to an end over time. The long-term goal should be to bring down debt-GDP ratio to 28 per cent each for the centre and states.

Sharing of Union Tax Revenues

— The share of states in the net proceeds of shareable central taxes fixed at 30.5 per cent, treating additional excise duties in lieu of sales tax as part of the general pool of central taxes. Share of states to come down to 29.5 per cent, when states are allowed to levy sales tax on sugar, textiles and tobacco.

— In case of any legislation enacted in respect of service tax, after the notification of the 88th amendment to the Constitution, revenue accruing to a state should not be less than the share that would accrue to it, had the entire service tax proceeds been part of the shareable pool.

— The indicative amount of overall transfers to states to be fixed at 38 per cent of the centre's gross revenue receipts.

— A grant of Rs. 20,000 crore for the panchayati raj institutions and Rs. 5,000 crore for the urban local bodies to be given to states for the period 2005-10.

— Priority will be given to expenditure on operation and maintenance costs of water supply and sanitation. For the scheme of solid waste management at least 50 per cent of the grants recommended for urban local bodies will be earmarked.

— Calamity Relief Fund will continue in its present form with contributions from the centre and states in the ratio of 75:25. The size of the fund for the period 2005-10 worked out at Rs. 21,333 crore.

— The outgo from the fund to be replaced by way of collection of National Calamity Contingent Duty. The definition of natural calamity will include landslides, avalanches, cloud bursts and pest attacks.

— Provision for disaster preparedness and mitigation to be part of state plans and not calamity relief.

Grants-in-aid to States

— Centre will confine itself to extending plan grants and leave it to states to decide its borrowings and the present system of central assistance for state plans to be done away with.

— Non-plan revenue deficit grant of Rs. 56,856 crore recommended to 15 states for the period 2005-10. Grants amounting to Rs. 10,172 crore for the education sector to eight states. Grants amounting to Rs.5,887 crore recommended for the health sector for seven states. Grants to education and health sectors are additionalities over and above the normal expenditure to be incurred by states.

— A grant of Rs.15,000 crore to be recommended for roads and bridges, which is in addition to the normal expenditure of grants recommended for maintenance of public buildings, forests, heritage conservation and specific needs of states are Rs. 500 crore , Rs. 1000 crore, Rs. 625 crore and Rs. 7,100 crore respectively.

Fiscal Reform Facility

— The Fiscal Reform Facility will not continue over the period 2005-10, with the recommended scheme of debt relief in place.

Debt Relief and Corrective Measures

— Central loans to states contracted till March 2004 and outstanding on March 31, 2005 amounting to Rs. 128,795 crore to be consolidated and rescheduled for a fresh term of 20 years, and an interest of 7.5 per cent to be charged on them. This is subject to enactment of fiscal responsibility legislation by a state.

— Introduction of a debt write-off scheme linked to reduction of revenue deficit of states. Under this scheme, repayments due from 2005-06 to 2009-10 on central loans contracted up to March 31, 2004 will be eligible for write-off.

— Central government not to act as an intermediary for future lending to states, except in the case of weak states, which are unable to raise funds from the market.

— External assistance to be transferred to states on the same terms and conditions as attached to such assistance by external funding agencies.

— All the states to set up sinking funds for amortisation of all loans.

— States to setup guarantee redemption funds through earmarked guarantee fees.

— The centre should share 'profit petroleum' from new exploration and licensing policy areas in the ratio of 50:50 with states where mineral oil and natural gas are produced. Profits will not be shared in respect of nomination fields and non-NELP blocks.

— Every state to set up a high level committee to monitor the utilisation of grants recommended by the TFC.

— The centre will gradually move towards the accrual basis of accounting.

Pay Commission

It is an administrative system/mechanism that the Government of India set up in 1956 to determine the salaries of government employees.

The first pay commission was established in 1956 and since then every decade has seen the birth of a commission that decides the wages of the government employees for a particular time-frame. For instance: fourth pay commission: 1986-1996, the fifth pay commission: - 1996 and this year.

Fifth Pay Commission Report and National Wage Policy

The fifth pay commission submitted its report on January 31, 1996, reducing the number of pay scales from 51 to 34. The commission has then prescribed the minimum and maximum salary which was fixed on the basis of the criteria suggested by the National Productivity Council and the commission arrived at a figure of Rs. 2,440 as the minimum salary for a government employee. For fixing the maximum salary an opinion survey pertaining to the present consumption level of the senior functionaries (joint secretaries and above) in government was conducted to ascertain what additionally they expected to meet their legitimate expenses. The pay commission accepted a figure of Rs. 26,000 for the secretaries to the Government of India.

By comparing the existing total emoluments (basic pay, dearness allowance plus interim relief) it was found that percentage increase works out to 8.8 per cent in the scale of Rs.750-

940 and 41.1 per cent in the scale of Rs.7,600-8,000. For the cabinet secretary the revision works out to be the highest at 48.7 per cent the highest among all the pay scales.

But if we include City Compensatory Allowance (CCA) and the House Rent Allowance (HRA) the gross salary of the lowest paid employee increases by 34.6 per cent and highest paid cabinet secretary by 84.8 per cent. This in view of the fact that the commission has permitted 30 per cent HRA for all categories irrespective of salary in class A cities.

Similarly the promotional policies and the rate of increments provided in various pay scales further increase the gap between the employees at the higher level.

A closer analysis of the recommendations of the fifth pay commission reveals that no scientific criteria were adopted for minimum and maximum pay fixation. The recommendations of the commission to revise HRA at the rate of 30 per cent of the basic salary and to provide 100 per cent neutralisation of inflation by providing corresponding rise in dearness allowance for all categories has helped to widen disparities between A grade and B, C and D grade service groups. The inescapable conclusion emerges that the fifth pay commission has followed an inverted concept of social justice. The report of the commission will thus not help in the evolution of a national wage policy reducing inequalities. While this will happen in the public sector, the problem will become worse if we also take into account the wages paid in the organised and unorganised private sector.

Appendix

World Trade Organisation (WTO)

The General Agreement on Tariffs and Trade (GATT), the predecessor of WTO, was born in 1948 as result of the international desire to liberalise trade.

The Bretton Woods Conference of 1944, which had recommended the IMF and World Bank, had also recommended the establishment of an International Trade Organisation (ITO). Although the IMF and World Bank were established in 1946, the ITO charter was never ratified, because of objections that its enforcement provisions would interfere with the autonomy of domestic policymaking. Instead, the GATT, which had been drawn up only as an interim agreement to fill the gap until the ITO charter was ratified, became the framework for international trading system since it came into being in 1948. The international trading system since 1948 was, at least in principle, guided by the rules and procedures agreed to by the signatories to the GATT which was an agreement signed by the contracting nations which were admitted on the basis of their willingness to accept GATT principles.

Following the UR Agreement, GATT was converted from a provisional agreement into a formal International organisation called World Trade Organisation (WTO) with effect from January 1, 1995. WTO now serves as a single institutional framework encompassing GATT and all the results of the Uruguay Round. It is directed by a Ministerial Conference that will meet at least once every two years and its regular business is overseen by a General Council.

GATT Rounds of Negotiations

The GATT was the only multilateral instrument governing international trade from 1948 until the WTO was established in 1995. Despite attempts in the mid 1950s and 1960s to create some form of institutional mechanism for international trade, the GATT continued to operate for almost half a century as a semi-institutionalised multilateral treaty regime on a provisional basis.

From Geneva to Tokyo

Seven rounds of negotiations occurred under the GATT before the first GATT trade rounds concentrated on further reducing tariffs. Then, the Kennedy Round in the mid- sixties brought about a GATT anti-dumping Agreement and a section on development. The Tokyo Round during the seventies was the first major attempt to tackle trade barriers that do not take the form of tariffs, and to improve the system, adopting a series of agreements on non-tariff barriers, which in some cases interpreted existing GATT rules, and in others broke entirely new ground. Because these plurilateral agreements were not accepted by the full GATT membership, they were often informally called "codes". Several of these codes were amended in the Uruguay Round, and turned into multilateral commitments accepted by all WTO members. Only four remained plurilateral (those on government procurement, bovine meat, civil aircraft and dairy products), but in 1997 WTO members agreed to terminate the bovine meat and dairy agreements, leaving only two.

Uruguay Round

Well before GATT's 40th anniversary, its members concluded that the GATT system was straining to adapt to a new globalising world economy. In response to the problems identified in the 1982 Ministerial Declaration (structural deficiencies, spill-over impacts of certain countries' policies on world trade GATT could not manage etc.), the eighth GATT round -known as the Uruguay Round - was launched in September 1986, in Punta del Este, Uruguay. It was the biggest negotiating mandate on trade ever agreed: the talks were going to extend the trading system into several new areas, notably trade in services and intellectual property, and to reform trade in the sensitive sectors of agriculture and textiles; all the original GATT articles were up for review.

The round was supposed to end in December 1990, but the US and EU disagreed on how to reform agricultural trade and decided to extend the talks. Finally, In November 1992, the US and EU settled most of their differences in a deal known informally as "the Blair House accord", and on April 15, 1994, the deal was signed by ministers from most of the 123 participating governments at a meeting in Marrakesh, Morocco. The agreement established the World Trade Organisation, which came into being upon its entry into force on January 1, 1995, and replaced GATT as an international organisation. It is widely regarded as the most profound institutional reform of the world trading system since the GATT's establishment.

The GATT still exists as the WTO's umbrella treaty for trade in goods, updated as a result of the Uruguay Round negotiations (a distinction is made between GATT 1994, the updated parts of GATT, and GATT 1947, the original agreement which is still the heart of GATT 1994). The GATT 1994 is not however the only legal agreement included in the Final Act; a long list of about 60 agreements, annexes, decisions and understandings was adopted. In fact, the agreements fall into a simple structure with six main parts: an umbrella agreement (the Agreement Establishing the WTO); agreements for each of the three broad areas of trade that the WTO covers (goods and investment (the Multilateral Agreements on Trade in Goods including the GATT 1994 and the TRIMS), services (GATS) and intellectual property (TRIPS); dispute settlement (DSU); and reviews of governments' trade policies (TPRM).

Doha Round

The WTO launched the current round of negotiations, the Doha Development Agenda (DDA) or Doha Round, at the Fourth Ministerial Conference in Doha, Qatar in November 2001. The Doha round was to be an ambitious effort to make globalisation more inclusive and help the world's poor, particularly by slashing barriers and subsidies in farming. The initial agenda comprised both further trade liberalisation and new rule-making, underpinned by commitments to strengthen substantially assistance to developing countries.

The talks have been highly contentious and agreement has not been reached, despite the intense negotiations at Fifth Ministerial Conference in Cancun in 2003 and at the Sixth Ministerial Conference in Hong Kong on December 13 - 18, 2005 and the Seventh Ministerial Conference in Geneva (July 2006). On July 24, 2006, at the end of yet another futile gathering of trade ministers in Geneva, Pascal Lamy, the WTO's Director-General, formally suspended the negotiations. This round of talks is yet to be concluded.

Functions of WTO

The WTO has the following five specific functions.

1. The WTO shall facilitate the implementation, administration and operation and further the objectives of the Multilateral Trade Agreements and shall also provide the framework for the implementation, administration and operation of plurilateral Trade Agreements.
2. The WTO shall provide the forum for negotiations among its members concerning their multilateral trade relations in matters dealt with under the Agreements.
3. The WTO shall administer the 'Understanding on Rules and Procedures Governing the Settlement of Disputes'
4. The WTO shall administer the 'Trade Review Mechanism'.
5. With a view to achieve greater coherence in global economic policymaking, the WTO shall cooperate, as appropriate, with the IMF and IBRD and its affiliated agencies.

The General Council will serve four main functions:

1. To supervise on a regular basis the operations of the revised agreements and ministerial declarations relating to (a) goods, (b) services and (c) TRIPs;
2. To act as a Dispute Settlement Body;
3. To serve as a Trade Review Mechanism; and
4. To establish Goods Council, Services Council and TRIPs Council, as subsidiary bodies.

The WTO is a more powerful body with enlarged functions than the GATT and is envisaged to play a major role in the world economic affairs. To become a member of the WTO, a country must completely accept the results of the Uruguay Round.

1. Liberalisation of Trade in Manufactures

Liberalisation of trade in manufactures is sought to be achieved mostly by reduction and phasing out of non-tariff barriers.

Tariff Barriers: The major liberalisations in respect of trade in manufactures, regarding tariffs, are:

1. Expansion of tariff bindings
2. Reduction in the tariff rates
3. Expansion of duty-free access

The UR Agreement envisages substantial tariff reductions in both industrial and developing countries.

The main liberalisations by industrial countries include the expansion of tariff bindings -(i.e., commitment not to exceed a particular level of tariff) to cover 99 percent of imports, the expansion of duty-free access from 20 to 43 percent of imports, and the reduction of trade weighted average tariff by 40 percent, from 6.2 to 3.7 percent.

However, the gains to developing countries from the tariff cuts by industrial countries are less impressive. The reduction in the average tariffs on their exports to industrial markets is 30 percent -and the labour intensive manufactures (textiles, clothing, leather goods) and certain processed primary products (fish products), which are, regarded as sensitive have below average tariff cuts.

In industrial countries, tariffs will be eliminated in several sectors like steel, pharmaceuticals and wood and wood products.

Developing countries agreed to bind their tariffs on 61 percent of their imports of industrial products, compared with 13 percent before the UR Round. They also offered to reduce their trade-weighted average bound tariff on imports from industrial countries by 28 percent, from 15 to 11 percent. The offers of tariff reduction on manufactures by developing countries are estimated to amount to over a third of the world total. The expansion of tariff binding by the developing countries, which rules out future increases in tariffs, is regarded as a significant achievement.

India has bound tariffs at 40 percent (where they were above 40 percent in 1993-94) on industrial raw materials, components and capital goods and at 25 percent in other cases. After the agreement comes into force, about 68 percent of India's tariff lines will be bound (compared to five percent earlier). In comparison, many developing countries in Asia and Latin America have bound between 90 and 100 percent of their tariff lines at levels comparable to, or lower than, India's bindings.

Non-tariff Barriers: In the area of NTBs, the Agreements to abolish voluntary export restraints (VERs) and to phase out the Multifibre Arrangements (MFA) are regarded as landmark achievements for developing countries.

The phasing out of the existing VERs within four years and the MFA within ten years would scale back the coverage of NTBs on developing countries' trade from 18 percent of their 1992 exports. As trade in derestricted product lines would tend to grow faster than other trade, this coverage could fall to 4.2 percent by 2005.

The UR Agreement seeks to phase out the MFA by 2005. According to some estimates the phasing out of MFA would contribute about 20 percent of the total welfare gains from the UR. The largest gains will go to the MFA importers who will be able to import basic clothing and textiles from the more efficient suppliers in ASEAN, China, South Asia and other regions. By 2005, the total benefits to the European Community, the US and Canada are estimated at $56 billion per year at 1992 prices. Income gains of over $13 billion are projected for highly competitive exporters such as China, Indonesia, Thailand and South Asian exporters, despite the loss of quota rents provided under the MFA. Some less competitive exporters will suffer from the loss of their preferential access to industrial country markets unless they are able to increase their efficiency, and some currently unrestricted importers will lose as the exports currently diverted toward them by restrictions elsewhere can flow freely to the other markets.

2. Liberalisation of Agricultural Trade

One of the salient features of the UR was the inclusion, for the first time, was the inclusion of agriculture in the MTN. The exclusion of agriculture from the previous Rounds and its effective exemption from the GATT discipline made agriculture a highly protected sector in the developed countries. The depressing impact of this on world prices prevented efficient producers from realising the benefits of their comparative advantage. Developing country exports suffered a lot.

The important aspects of the UR Agreement on agriculture include.

1. Tariffication
2. Tariff binding
3. Tariff cuts
4. Reduction in subsidies and domestic support.

Tariffication and Tariff Cuts: Tariffication means the replacement of existing non-tariff restrictions on trade such as import quotas by such tariffs as would provide substantially the same level of protection.

From the first year of the Agreement's implementation, nearly all border protection is to be examined by tariffs, which (in principle) are to be no higher than the tariff equivalent of the protection levels prevailing in the base periods.

Industrial countries are then to reduce their tariff bindings by an average of 36 percent within six years (from 1995) while all developing countries but the poorest are required to reduce by an average of 24 percent over a period of ten years. Least developed countries are not required to make any commitment for reduction of tariffs on agricultural products.

Subsidies and Domestic Support Policies: The UR Agreement deals with three categories of subsidies.

1. *Prohibited subsidies*—those contingent upon export performance or the use of instead of imported goods.
2. *Actionable subsidies*—those that have demonstrably adverse effects on other member countries.
3. *Non-actionable subsidies*—including those provided (with stipulated limitations) to industrial research and procompetitive development activity to disadvantaged regions, or to existing facilities to adapt themselves to new environmental requirements.

Non-Agricultural Export Subsidies

Countries whose per capita income is less than $1000 are not bound to phase out export subsidies. However, even such countries will have to phase out export subsidies on products where the share in the world exports is 3.25 percent or more in two consecutive years. This is applicable to India in respect to export of diamonds.

Bibliography

1. Todaro and Smith, *Economic Development*, 8th Edition.
2. Meier, *Leading Issues in Economic Development*, 6th Edition.
3. S. Chakravarti, *Development Planning: The Indian Experience.*
4. Tenth Plan, Vol. I.
5. Rangarajan, C., *The New Economic Policy and the Role of the State.*
6. Deepak Nayyar, "Economic Growth in Independent India", *Economic and Political Weekly*, April 15, 2006.
7. Minhas, B.S., "Public Vs Private Sector", in Uma Kapila's *Indian Economy since Independence*, 17th Edition.
8. Rangarajan C., *Disinvestment: Strategies and Issues.*
9. Jermoni, P.D., *Foreign Direct Investment in India—Trends and Impact.*
10. Government of India, Economy Survey 2004-2005.
11. Rangarajan C., *India's Balance of Payments: The Emerging Dimensions.*
12. Srinivasan, T. N., "Foreign Trade Policies and India's Development", reproduced in Uma Kapila's *Indian Economy since Independence.*
13. Datt and Sundharam, *Indian Economy*, 52nd Edition.

Index